D0771375

T1-BLH-827

ALSO
BY
MICHAEL LEWIS

LIAR'S POKER: RISING
THROUGH THE WRECKAGE
ON WALL STREET

THE LARGER AGENDA SERIES

PACIFIC RIFT

MICHAEL LEWIS

WHITTLE DIRECT BOOKS

Photographs: Bob Collins by Neil Krivonak/Clique, page 8; Captain Munakata by Neil Krivonak/Clique, page 29; Karel van Wolferen (self-portrait), page 40; James Fallows, Bret Littlehales, page 42; Bob Collins at the Tokyo American Club by Neil Krivonak/Clique, page 46; Shuji Tomikawa by Laura Levine, page 52; Shuji and Yuki Tomikawa by Laura Levine, page 78; W. Edwards Deming, Shonna Valeska, page 80.

Library of Congress Catalog Number: 90-71779
Lewis, Michael
Pacific Rift
ISBN 0-9624745-6-8
ISSN 1046-364X

The Larger Agenda Series

The Larger Agenda Series presents original short books by distinguished authors on subjects of importance to managers and policymakers in business and the public sector.

The series is edited and published by Whittle Communications L.P., an independent publishing company. A new book appears approximately every other month. The series reflects a broad spectrum of responsible opinions. In each book the opinions expressed are those of the author, not the publisher or the advertiser.

I welcome your comments on this unique endeavor.

William S. Rukeyser
Editor in Chief

CONTENTS

INTRODUCTION

wenty years ago it would have been strange for a young American without a special interest in Japan to do business with a Japanese. These days every young American I know seems to have had the experience. My own first exposure to Japan came five years ago on the London trading floor where I sold bonds for the American investment bank Salomon Brothers. By the time I first encountered Japanese in the marketplace, they had a well-earned reputation for being as reluctant as a nun on a date. Only after months of dinners, phone calls, and countless meetings over charts and graphs would they give you business. And even then you might come away empty-handed. The only sure way to sell bonds to a Japanese money manager, I was told, was to lead him to believe that every other Japanese money manager was buying from you. Nothing moved a Japanese so surely as the fear of being left behind.

As we bond salesmen plumbed the shallows of the Japanese mind, the finances of America and Japan were growing together. Every three months the U.S. Treasury announced its intention to borrow $10 billion or so, and every three months thousands of Americans looked at each other and asked the same question: "Will the Japanese buy?" Every three months a rumor circulated that the Japanese had lost interest in financing the American deficit. Every three months this rumor would cause the American government-bonds market to collapse. Then the Japanese would start to buy. Quickly. For when Japanese money moved, it moved all at once; and we felt certain that the behavior of Japanese money was being coordinated by some sinister force.

A lot has been written about commercial relations between Japan and America. The tendency of the writers has been to emphasize the absence of borders in the modern world. What with the relatively free flow of money and goods and advances in communications, national distinctions are being rendered meaningless. On some level this may be true. But nations still levy taxes, impose trade quotas, and declare wars. And to an American sitting at a desk in Europe, trying to do business with Japanese, national distinctions—or more precisely, cultural traits—were becoming more rather than less important. I had never before seen so much chaos and misunderstanding. This was the start of my curiosity about Japan.

By the time I left Salomon Brothers, I had assembled a long list of questions, most of which touched upon the current friction between Japan and America. Why did the Japanese persist in piling up massive trade and capital surpluses? Why did they throw good money after bad into the American bond market and appear indifferent to losing fortunes? Why was one investment bank, Salomon Brothers, raking in hundreds of millions of dollars in Japan when its otherwise worthy competitors could not gain a toehold? Why, if Japanese financial institutions like Mitsui and Mitsubishi were coordinating their activities, did they also loathe one another so obviously?

In satisfying my own curiosity, I hoped to address the principal source of tension between America and Japan: the mistrust with which each views the other's motives and methods. Most of what has been written on the subject of Japan's threat to America has been of a political orientation filtered through politicians and trade negotiators. This is odd, since the main characters in the conflict between Japan and America are businessmen. Probably the reason for the gap between literature and reality is that businessmen are shy of the press. So it seemed useful to go in search of business people who would talk—real people in the midst of the fray, who could answer my questions about what it's like to conduct business in a foreign culture.

My plan was to find and describe an American businessman in Japan and a Japanese businessman in America. I intended to write more *around* them than about them; I envisioned them as leads in a Pacific soap opera that had been running since Japanese and Americans first encountered one another 150 years ago. What I needed was people who would let me tag along while they worked, tell me what they really thought, introduce me to their friends and colleagues, and send me off to read books whenever I asked a stupid question. And I had a lot of stupid questions to ask.

"I help Delacre cookies batter the competition."

Doug Hottel
Worldwide Account Executive, Brussels, Belgium

For the Campbell Soup Company and its Belgian subsidiary, Biscuits Delacre,
Federal Express is an essential ingredient in their pan-European marketing recipe.
Delacre uses Federal Express international delivery service to ship new products from
Belgium for testing at Campbell's research center in the U.S. which enables them to
cut product development time. And deliver their cookies to market faster.
A competitive advantage that can be particularly sweet.

1

JAPANESE DEFENSE

*"When it is not necessary to change, it is necessary
not to change."*

—Lucius Cary (c. 1610-1643),
Viscount of Falkland

The first American tourist to set foot on Japanese soil was locked into a cage. His name was Ranald MacDonald (spelled differently but pronounced the same as the patron saint of hamburgers). More than 100 years before the fast-food chain was founded, the MacDonalds of Oregon developed a fascination for Japan. Ranald was seized by the perverse conviction that he had Japanese blood, though his mother was of Indian ancestry. In 1848, at the age of 20, he booked passage on a whaling ship scheduled to cruise by northern Japan. When the ship neared the coast, young Ranald pushed off in a dinghy and began to paddle. He feared, rightly, that if he arrived by boat his Japanese cousins would simply shove him back out to sea. So before hitting the beaches, he capsized the dinghy and floated ashore on the trunk containing his belongings. It could have been then—when the white man on the trunk first came into view— that the Japanese conceived of the human cage.

The cage, made of wood, was sent to Edo (the former name of Tokyo), where it sat with its disillusioned captive on display for several weeks. Although American sailors had washed up from time to time on the shores of northern Japan, the citizens of Edo had never before seen an American. Japan had been off-limits to foreigners for more than 200 years, and the few foreigners required for trade were confined on a tiny island off the southern coast called Dejima. (An anonymous 19th-century Dutch author explained in *Manners and Customs of the Japanese in the Nineteenth*

Century that "when the Japanese government began to entertain a jealousy and dislike of foreigners, the first measure taken was to place them where they could conveniently be watched.")

So it was to Dejima that the Japanese authorities wheeled the cage containing Ranald MacDonald. There he was released from the cage and there he remained, teaching English to a few budding Japanese internationalists, until a ship arrived that was willing to return him to America.

The island was central to the concept I shall be calling the Japanese Defense. When using this term, I am referring to the pattern of Japan's domestic, social, and economic arrangements, which hadn't changed in 200 years. The power of the Tokugawa shogunate had been preserved at all costs. Since the shogun viewed any change of the status quo as a threat, change was outlawed. Meddling foreign missionaries and disruptive Japanese were put to death. Foreign merchants and adventurers were locked into cages or confined to Dejima. The essence of the Japanese Defense was (and is) maintaining the status quo.

Probably Ranald MacDonald would have been forgotten entirely had one of his former students not been present to interpret when another American, Commodore Matthew C. Perry, came to Japan five years later bearing letters from President Millard Fillmore. Perry had four warships, a mission to open Japan to trade and diplomatic relations with the U.S., and an approach to his task that was slightly more informed than MacDonald's. He had read *Manners and Customs*, and he'd spoken with knowledgeable Dutchmen. Unlike many of the Americans who arrived in his wake, Perry correctly diagnosed the Japanese penchant for bold and dramatic displays of authority. So before sailing into Edo, he rehearsed with his 560 crew members a tableau in which they threw themselves facedown on the deck in preparation for his appearance before the Japanese emperor. If his greatest fear was that the emperor would ignore him, his greatest anxiety was that word of this little skit would reach home and he would be ridiculed in the press.

The first recorded Japanese-American conversation took place as Perry entered Edo Bay. Irritated Japanese darted out in tiny boats to meet the black warships and express their displeasure. One Japanese waved a sign that said GO AWAY! DO NOT DARE TO ANCHOR! From another came the surprising question (in Dutch): "Are you the Americans?" *How*, Perry wondered, *did they know?* Once he'd recovered from the shock of being recognized, the commodore set about to meet the emperor. Descriptions of his efforts, were they compiled into a case study at

After the failure of his entrepreneurial scheme to import cows to Japan, Bob Collins learned never to jump into the waters of the Japanese "system" without a life ring.

Harvard Business School, might be titled "How to See the Chairman of the Board Without an Appointment."

In his book *The House of Mitsui*, published in 1939, Oland Russell wrote, "The first minor Japanese official who appeared was permitted to converse only with one of Perry's low-ranking officers. Perry himself kept out of sight. The Japanese sent out an officer of higher rank. This man got only one step up with the

Americans. A vice-governor rated a flag lieutenant; the governor rated a captain, and so on. The Japanese were agreeably surprised. The barbarian lord apparently knew how to do things. Previous visitors had been trying to send mere orderlies to see the emperor. . . . The plan worked to perfection. Within 10 days, a prince with imperial credentials was on hand."

Perry brought a letter from President Fillmore requesting trade and diplomatic relations. He told the Japanese that he would be back in a few months to sort out a treaty. Then he left. Whereupon the Japanese began to hope they'd seen the last of the man with the big guns. They hadn't. When Perry returned the following year, he came with not four warships but seven, as well as a list of demands in the form of a trade treaty. The Japanese, face to face for the first time in more than two centuries with a hostile superior military force, had no choice but to grant the Americans supplies for their ships, rights for their shipwrecked sailors, and two strips of land on which to build ports. The first Japanese-American treaty has to be considered, together with the American Occupation after World War II, as one of the two worst defeats ever inflicted upon those Japanese who feel that the precious, mysterious quality of their country is threatened by prolonged contact with the outside world. The foreigners had established a beachhead, and it was only a matter of time before they pushed inland.

The Americans, for their part, felt a surging self-righteousness as they sensed the inevitable spread of the American way. "We are comforted," wrote President Fillmore in a puff-chested letter to the Japanese emperor, "by the reflection that his Japanese majesty was not offended by the manly, yet respectful, frankness of our republican chief." And in his journal, Perry wrote, "It seems not altogether inappropriate that the United States should be the instrument of breaking down these barriers and of opening Japan to the rest of the World."

Hear, hear.

RANALD RIDES AGAIN

Anyone who has seen one of the 17 (and counting) Japanese-produced Godzilla movies has also seen, in miniature, the Japanese view of the world. To a Japanese, the world is an accident waiting to happen—to him. It is a collection of powerful, uncontrollable forces that are forever rising out of land and sea to squash Japanese executives flat as compact discs. This collective mental melodrama is not without some justification. As the Japanese never tire of telling, their country has had more than its fair share of earthquakes, typhoons, tidal waves, and volcanos. For the last four centuries Tokyo has been leveled by quakes every 70 or so years: 1633, 1703, 1782, 1853, 1923. It seems that every day in Japan some unsuspecting Japanese drives his car into a volcano or is swept off a beach by a wave. THREE DROWNED BY WAVE IN PREFECTURE was one of the first Japanese headlines I ever saw. Personally, I have yet to understand why, when a Japanese is walking down the beach and sees a big wave coming, he doesn't just step aside like they do on the New Jersey shore. But there you have it: a genuine cultural difference. There is a natural place in Japan for an insurance executive.

Robert J. Collins spent 11 years of his life trying to sell insurance to Japanese companies. Until he quit in 1988, he managed the corporate-insurance division of one of America's most successful insurers, the American International Group (AIG). For those 11 years he was one of six Westerners in a company of 2,500 Japanese. During that time he also served as president of the board of the Nishimachi International School, started a company to advise Japanese investors in America, founded a new private school where he served as dean of admissions, and became one of the few non-Japanese board members of the Tokyo Lawn Tennis Club, where he occasionally played doubles with Emperor Akihito. ("It's not easy," he has said, "to lob a god.") With his dark suit, white shirt, and buzz-sawed hair, Collins looks deceptively like a boring, early-middle-aged American executive. Somewhere along the way, however, someone forgot to tell him how an insurance salesman was meant to behave. The truth is that he has a special knack for making trouble, for which I was deeply grateful. After a couple of months of library research, I had come to see the story of American visits to Japan as a series of tragicomic misunderstandings in the spirit of Ranald Mac-Donald. Collins was very much a part of this tradition—to the point that when I write about him I imagine him, like his predecessor, floating toward some Japanese beach on a trunk. His unusual approach to life has led him to learn firsthand the ways in which Japan defends itself.

Bob Collins's first encounter with a Japanese occurred in the early 1960s in upper Illinois. He found himself, in his English class at Rockford College, staring at the back of a lovely Japanese girl's head. Being from a Japanese family of high social standing, Keiko Okamura sat primly in the front row and took good notes. Being a member of the Rockford College basketball team, Collins sat in the back and made farting noises with his armpits. He recalls his unlikely first encounter with Keiko: "I saw her reading this letter from home, and it was written in kanji. I'd seen kanji signs, but I'd never seen anything handwritten. I couldn't believe people actually wrote like that. So I was looking over her shoulder, and she was pulling the letter away so I couldn't see—like I could have understood what it said!" When exam time came, Collins asked to borrow Keiko's notes—a habit he would never quite break. She complied. Two years later he was on a plane to Tokyo for their wedding.

"That was my first trip to Japan," he says. "I landed and got off the plane, and the first thing I notice is that there are all these construction workers all over the place. It was 1963, and Japan was getting ready to host the Olympics. The thing that struck me was the construction workers in their hard hats and helmets. I'd seen pictures of soldiers fighting in the jungle in Southeast Asia; I'd seen all the John Wayne movies with Japanese soldiers wearing the same kind of uniforms. I get off the airplane and I'm surrounded by them. So my first impression was that I was in an armed camp, surrounded by soldiers."

The newlyweds returned to New York, where by night Collins wrote soap operas for television and blurbs and prefaces to Signet Classics. If in the late 1960s you happened upon a paperback edition of *Tristram Shandy*, *Treasure Island*, or *Anna Karenina* and saw emblazoned on its cover something like "The tension between good and evil is the theme that occupied Tolstoy throughout his life," then you have probably read the unsigned work of Robert J. Collins.

"I was what you'd call a hack," Collins says. "The tension between good and evil—that was my idea."

By day, however, Collins was making an assault on the top of the American insurance business. He began his career in 1962 as a salesman for Continental Casualty (later CNA Insurance) and rose quickly. He opened a CNA branch in Washington, D.C., in 1966, then moved to Detroit in 1969 to manage the office there. In late 1971 he was hired by American International Group, where

"Try telling your kid you fly a warehouse for a living."

Mark McNair
Pilot, Indianapolis

By using Federal Express planes to deliver everything from computer parts
to airline tickets just when they're needed, companies are discovering that they can
keep inventory costs from soaring.

he ran a sales force in New York, then regional offices in Boston and Philadelphia. In 1977 he was transferred to AIG's Japanese subsidiary, American Insurance Underwriters (AIU), to manage a division in a company that was one of the few great foreign corporate success stories in Japan. Collins first drifted into the teeth of the Japanese Defense through a typically American entrepreneurial scheme. Like many of Collins's seemingly endless string of bizarre experiences in Japan, his first encounter had nothing to do with insurance. It had to do with meat.

From day one, Collins had been upset by the price of steak in Japan. The Japanese had long treated beef as a delicacy, increasing its price through a complex system of quotas and tariffs and a distribution system that seemed designed to maximize the number of hands through which a slab of raw meat passed before it could be barbecued. The Tokyo American Club, of which Collins was a board member, was paying through the nose for steak. "I was thinking, *There's gotta be a way to beat the system.* I was thinking that maybe the thing to do was import cattle. Cattle is not beef, so there wouldn't be any tariffs."

For an American, importing and raising cows in Japan required a certain leap of faith. Although Collins was raised outside Chicago and claims to have a sixth sense for the sort of things people do on farms, he had never had hands-on experience with cows. "Remember, I went to school at the University of Iowa," he says, neglecting to mention that he has lived most of his life in cities.

The first 150 cows were flown in by Northwest Airlines from northern Iowa and set to graze on Hokkaido, Japan's northernmost island. Collins is vague about how the head of an insurance company in Tokyo goes about finding cows. "I just knew a guy who knew a guy," he says. "They were probably hot, but that's another story."

"Hot cows?"

"Yeah, well, I'm not saying they were rustled, exactly. Anyway, there was no way anyone was going to trace them. I don't know if you know this, being from the city, but cows don't have fingerprints."

The original idea was that after the cows had a chance to "get over their jet lag," they'd be quartered and ferried to Tokyo. The Tokyo American Club had its own butcher shop and restaurant, where the sides of beef could be carved and served. The American Club sent several of its more rugged Japanese employees up to Hokkaido to become cowboys. There was, at first, only one small snag. Immediately upon their arrival, the cattle became ill from eating the dried rice stalks that form the staple of a Japanese cow's diet. American cows, like American businessmen, had trouble with the local cuisine. "It was cutting up their stomachs," explains Collins, knowledgeably. "We had to import alfalfa cubes from Montana." Dining on alfalfa cubes, the cows grew fat, and the price of steak at the American Club dropped by 20 percent. Collins's flaky idea was looking more and more like a triumph of American ingenuity over Japanese protectionism.

Then Japanese officialdom snooped. A belief in the omniscience of Japanese officialdom is central to the whole notion of the Japanese Defense. "They didn't know we were bringing the cows in to eat them, but when the cows started to disappear," says Collins, "they figured it out." What happened next is instructive for anyone contemplating any venture in Japan that disrupts the established order. There was no rule against importing live cattle. There was no rule preventing the American Club from eating its pets. There was nothing Japanese government officials could do . . . directly.

The beef trade in Japan is a closely held cartel vaguely associated in the Japanese mind with gangsters. Japanese beef distributors saw that the consumption by Americans of even a few stray cows was a threat to their hegemony. To this day, Collins remains shocked by the violence of the reaction. The first people affected were the Japanese cowboys sent to Hokkaido. Their wives were visited in their homes by thugs from the beef trade, who suggested that perhaps it was time for their husbands to return. "Once the beef trade started to threaten our other Japanese employees," says Collins, "we couldn't get anyone to cooperate. The guys in our butcher shop were refusing to carve up our own cows."

The end came when the Japanese suppliers of the American Club kitchen began to intentionally foul up their deliveries. "For example," says Collins, "for days we weren't getting supplied with chicken and vegetables. All we had was beef. The guys at the club would look down at their plates and say, 'Oh no, not another steak.'" The cow farm had become far more trouble than it was worth, so the few remaining cows were given away to Japanese farmers.

Collins claims he wasn't surprised that a combination of official intelligence and unofficial bullying had repelled his impish assault. He is quick to admit that the first rule in Japan is that the status quo is sacred. Yet he insisted as he finished his tale that Japan is penetrable by foreigners. "In retrospect, there are a lot of things we didn't do right," he says, although what those things might be he's not sure. In his frustration, Bob Collins is similar to virtually every American who has ever tried to do business in Japan; it is his delight in having tried and his reluctance to bear grudges that sets him apart.

Collins is ambivalent about the current fashion for criticism of Japanese exclusionary business practices. According to him, nearly all of the biggest American companies that have succeeded in Japan (Coca-Cola, IBM, NCR) have done so because they had a new product with not even an approximate precedent in Japan. "Most foreign success stories here," he says, "have been with products that can't be duplicated without violating patent rights. Even McDonald's falls into that category." When pressed, he could think of only one exception to his general rule about foreign success, but it was a big one: AIU.

A GRIPPING TALE OF INSURANCE

A mere branch of a U.S. parent company, AIU was, by the time Collins arrived, larger than all but 13 Japanese property-and-casualty insurance companies; by 1989 it was taking in 200 billion yen ($1.3 billion) a year in Japanese premiums, making it larger than all other foreign insurers combined. Two-thirds of the 3.5 percent market share controlled by foreign non-life companies belonged to AIU. Between a quarter and a third of all foreign revenues earned by AIU came from Japan. When a Japanese was swept off the beach in his Nissan, there was about a one-in-40 chance that AIU would end up paying for it. If Tokyo were reduced to rubble, AIU assessors would be sifting through it to settle claims. This, in insurance, is success, and AIU had enjoyed enough of it to be cited by spokesmen within the Japanese government as evidence of the country's openness.

To help explain how a company could be so much more successful in Japan than its American rivals, Collins called upon Dick Cropp, an expert on Japanese politics and business. From 1979 until early 1990, Cropp had been head of the American Chamber of Commerce, which represents the 560 U.S. companies in Japan. Together, Collins and Cropp explained the rules of the local insurance game, beginning with the role of the Japanese government.

The prices of all insurance policies in Japan are fixed by the Ministry of Finance (MOF). They are somewhere between two and five times the rates paid in America. Japanese consumers suffer because newcomers are prevented from winning business by undercutting the competition. This is a happy situation for the 20 established Japanese property-and-casualty insurers, most of which sit within comfortable walking distance of their protectors at the ministry. To achieve the same results at home, American insurance companies would have to collude on price, which, even if it were legal, would be difficult. There are more than 10,000 property-and-casualty insurance companies spread across America.

After price-fixing, the most important rule in the insurance game is that all new forms of coverage must be approved by the Ministry of Finance. A new kind of policy is often a source of great profits in the insurance business, as is a new product in any business. Because Western insurance companies have tended to be more innovative than their Japanese counterparts, a new policy would seem to be one of the most likely ways for them to gain entry into the Japanese market—in theory, anyway. "For years," says Dick Cropp, who has watched the process for almost two decades, "the MOF wouldn't let you bring in new policies. Then they relaxed a little. When Bob Collins, or whoever, wanted to bring in a new kind of policy, the ministry would take a look at it, study it, get committees together of the Japanese non-life insurance companies, and decide that, yes, that's a good policy to offer, and you may all offer it at the same time at such and such a price."

New ideas were automatically shared within the Japanese market. Cropp had been in Japan so long and had seen this kind of thing so often that he had forgotten his original indignation at this basic violation of the American notion of fair play. There was not a flicker of emotion on his face as he continued. "There has been only one exception," he said. "A company called American Family came to Japan in 1980 and offered a cancer policy. The Ministry of Finance took one look at it and said, 'Who the hell wants a cancer policy? Sure, go ahead.' It was the only time they blew it." At this, both Cropp and Collins fell about laughing.

"Is that a joke?" I asked.

American Family, they explained, has had a brilliant run with its policy, all because the Ministry of Finance thought it wouldn't succeed. The ministry was so certain of the policy's failure that it hadn't bothered instructing the other Japanese insurers about its nuances. The policy, according to industry experts, is unexceptional, and it caught fire in Japan only because, as Cropp and Collins put it, "the Japanese are hypochondriacs." If a foreign insurer broke into Japan in a big way, in other words, it was because the bureaucrats whose job it was to keep them out didn't anticipate the wants of their own people. Now *that* sounded like the sort of government I knew.

"I very quickly learned that pricing, underwriting judgment—all those things you are trained to do as an insurance man growing up—simply don't apply over here," said Collins. "My whole life was spent dreaming up how to improve service. You do service things for the customer that the Japanese can't or won't do. That's partly why AIU got started. In the U.S., the burden was on the insurer to disprove the claim. Here the contract itself wasn't prima facie evidence of anything. You had to walk in and *prove* that you should collect. So AIU came in here and said, 'Okay, your car fell off the Shuto Expressway and we have photos of it; we'll pay.' Whereas a Japanese company would say, 'Why you turn left? Why you upside down in rice field?'"

It is often said that Japanese companies are more sensitive to the needs of their customers than their Western counterparts, and for this reason they dominate world markets for cars, stereos, VCRs. Oddly, the one clear edge that Western insurance companies have is in customer service. They trust their customers. "Western auto-insurance policies," Collins explained, "state that the company will pay in the event of a wreck. Japanese auto policies say the same thing, but they also describe what is meant by 'a wreck.' 'Run into other car going same way'; 'Run into other car going opposite way'; 'Run into other car from side way'; 'Run off road into agricultural field'; 'Run off road into nonagricultural field'; 'Run into object not moving'; 'Run into standing person'; and so on. Running into, let's say, a space capsule that has somehow landed on the Shuto Expressway would cause significant consternation in the Japanese underwriting bullpen. The claim would be paid, but a great deal of wind-sucking would occur first, *and* an endorsement to the policy would have to be licensed in order to handle future contingencies of the same ilk ('Space capsules, space vehicles, space junk, etc.')."

So although the Ministry of Finance stripped Western insurance companies of their two greatest weapons, pricing and innovation, they can still put up a respectable fight with their user-friendly attitudes. Unfortunately, that raises as many questions as it answers. If Westerners have this natural advantage, why have they made so little progress? Why can't the American and European insurance companies that compete ferociously with AIU in other markets also compete in Japan? Even AIU's market share has been basically stable since the 1960s—stuck at 2.5 percent. Why isn't it expanding into the Japanese market with the same force as, say, Sony thrusts into America?

"Because of the way the system is constructed," said Cropp. "If you are a foreigner coming in to sell to a Japanese, and the Japanese normally buys from Watanabe, even if you are offering better service or a discount of 20 percent, he is going to work out some way that he can save Watanabe's ass before he buys your product. So . . . you're blocked."

"It's the system," Collins agreed.

If I had a dime for every time an American businessman mentioned "the system" while I was in Japan, I wouldn't be bothering to write about it now. A new school of political writers has come to use the phrase to describe the "balance between semiautonomous groups that share power" in Japan, including gangsters, ministry officials, bureaucrat-businessmen, agricultural cooperatives, the press, and the police. I came to think of the system as the American businessman's shorthand for the multitude of invisible barriers ranging from passive consumers to meddling bureaucrats. The barriers don't exist specifically to exclude foreigners but rather to preserve the status quo. The system may be the enemy of the outsider, but only because preserving the status quo naturally entails rebuffing all newcomers, Japanese or foreign.

The system is as egalitarian in whom it includes as it is in whom it excludes; it protects the small as well as the large. The Japanese insurance market is a case in point. Of the 20 domestic companies, five are giants that control about 65 percent of the entire market. Excepting the 3.5 percent taken by foreigners, the rest of the market is divided among 15 smaller companies. A thrust by AIU (or any other outsider) would either reduce the shares of small insurance companies or challenge the monsters.

"Why not drive the little guys out of business," I asked Collins and Cropp, "like they do in America?"

"The first rule in Japan," said Collins, "is that no one is allowed to go out of business." (This was later echoed by an official at the Japanese insurance guild. When I asked him the same question, he looked like he wanted to slap my wrist with a ruler. "Here in Japan," he said, "no bankruptcies.") "Everybody has a niche," said Collins. "Everybody's settled; everybody's got a place."

The streets of Japan are cluttered with evidence supporting

Collins's claim: there is an abundance of mom-and-pop stores of the type long ago dispatched in America by supermarkets; two-bit noodle shops that have been in business for 40 years occupy the ground floors of the newest skyscrapers; rice paddies flourish in the middle of Tokyo's business district. The insurance industry is no exception. When a small Japanese insurer has trouble, the Ministry of Finance steps in and assigns executives from one of the bigger firms to sort it out. The bigger firms comply not because they love the little ones but because they, too, are dependent upon the ministry's defense of the status quo.

Much of the ministry's mental energy is spent avoiding such problems. "I go over to the Ministry of Finance on behalf of AIU," says Collins, "and ask to introduce a new policy. The guy across the table from me can understand why I want to do it, and he'll say 'Yes, I understand.' But what he's asking himself in the back of his mind is: *What about those bottom 15 companies? Can they even handle that kind of insurance? Is this going to jeopardize them?*"

This isn't merely discrimination against foreigners, says Collins, but discrimination against anyone who tries to change the status quo. In spite of the fat margins available in the fixed-price market, no new domestic insurance company has been formed in Japan for 13 years. That's because the Ministry of Finance, which passes out insurance licenses, knows that new entrants cause trouble.

It seems sort of un-American not to be able to bury the little guys. I was willing, however, to accept this as given. But what about the big companies? The five giant firms are Tokio Marine & Fire, Taisho Marine & Fire, Sumitomo Marine & Fire, Nippon Fire & Marine, and Yasuda Fire & Marine. The market share of each has remained virtually fixed for nearly 40 years, and the companies are ranked by the day they were founded. Tokio Marine & Fire, a Mitsubishi group company and the first Japanese property-and-casualty insurer (founded in 1879), is the largest collector of premiums, followed by Yasuda Fire & Marine, Taisho Marine & Fire (which will change its name in April 1991 to Mitsui Marine & Fire), and Sumitomo Marine & Fire. I spoke with many insurance men—Japanese as well as foreign—who regard this preternatural stability as prima facie evidence that the market is apportioned by the Ministry of Finance. How else could the rankings remain so stable?

Part of Collins's job as the boss of AIU's corporate-insurance

"It's 3 a.m.
Do you know where your package is? I do."

Dennis Connelly
Trace Agent, Boston

No matter what time of day or night you need to know about your packages,
documents, or freight—no matter where on earth they may be—our tracking networks
allow our Customer Service Agents to track them down for you. In seconds.

division was to sell to the group companies of Mitsubishi, Mitsui, Sumitomo, and Yasuda. Here he was playing into the strength of the Japanese Defense, and he realized pretty quickly that he was wasting his time. There were longstanding historical ties within the groups, reinforced by old-school ties (each group has its affiliated university), intermarriage, nepotism, networks of indebtedness, cross-holdings of shares, and countless group nights out in Tokyo Ginza hostess bars. Since Mitsubishi Bank, Mitsubishi Corporation, and Mitsubishi Trust are the largest shareholders in Tokio Marine & Fire, it isn't terribly surprising that they purchase their corporate insurance from the company. As a U.S. congressional official told *Business Week*, "The conspiracies form naturally within the *keiretsu* [corporate groups], and they are conducted informally. Word of mouth is sacred. Nobody breaks the deal."

Some people, such as this U.S. official, use the term *keiretsu* interchangeably with *zaibatsu*. I prefer *zaibatsu* for the *inter*market groups and *keiretsu* for the *intra*market groups. There is a distinction worth making here between these two corporate groups. The intramarket groups usually form around a single large industrial company that operates in a single market, such as Toyota in automobiles or Matsushita in electronics, and consist of several subsidiaries and subsidiaries' affiliates subservient to the parent. The intermarket groups, such as Mitsubishi and Mitsui, are seemingly random clusters of supposedly independent companies, linked by shared traditions. Of the Big Six intermarket groups (Mitsubishi, Mitsui, Sumitomo, Fuyo-Yasuda, Sanwa, Dai-Ichi Kangyo), four (Mitsubishi, Mitsui, Sumitomo, and Fuyo-Yasuda) are holdovers of the Big Four *zaibatsu*—huge combines of unrelated businesses controlled by family-owned holding companies—that, in theory, were dissolved during the American Occupation. Two (Mitsubishi and Fuyo-Yasuda) have their roots in the mid-19th century, and two more (Mitsui and Sumitomo) date back to the middle of the 17th century.

Although this is not the place for a complete history of the *zaibatsu,* a few things do need to be said. The first is that the clubby feeling in the Japanese economy grew, paradoxically, out of divisions in Japanese society in the middle of the last century. Whether the feudal empires mushroomed in response to the shock of having to deal frankly with Americans or were merely the inevitable consequence of trends under way long before the foreigners arrived remains a matter of historical debate. In either case, soon after the signing of Perry's treaty with Japan, a coup d'état politely known as the Meiji Restoration occurred. It transferred power from the shogun to an elite civil service, the ancestor of the present Japanese bureaucracy.

The samurai-bureaucrats who ran Japan, when faced with the problem of building an economy to compete with the Western powers, began to inject capital into the few large and intensely competitive merchant groups. "Many attempts had been made to organize merchants and other wealthy men into companies serving the state's economic policies," wrote John Roberts in his authoritative biography of the Mitsui company. "But the spirit of cooperation was slow to develop among them. . . . Until a more liberal and enlightened business community could be developed, only centralized, dictatorial establishments could overcome those difficulties. It was on the basis of these stark necessities and limited options that the *zaibatsu*, those uniquely Japanese agglomerates that themselves became the massive building blocks of Japan's state capitalism, were erected."

It is also important to realize that the *zaibatsu*, according to the economic historian William Lockwood, were never monopolies in the conventional sense. Although it was based upon giant family-owned businesses, Japan's new capitalism bore only a faint resemblance to the American economy at the turn of the century, when companies such as U.S. Steel and Standard Oil were able to control 65 to 95 percent of output in their fields. The new Japanese markets in trading, shipbuilding, and banking were fiercely competitive oligopolies dominated by the holding companies of the family-owned *zaibatsu*.

The third thing worth knowing about the prewar *zaibatsu* is that, although they grew most rapidly during booms, they consolidated their social position during busts. The *zaibatsu* banks survived while their smaller rivals failed. The single most important advantage of the *zaibatsu* was and still is their control of finance (including insurance), which allowed them access to capital when capital was scarce. They absorbed smaller firms in crises, of which there were plenty in the years leading up to World War II. By 1944 Mitsubishi controlled 25 percent of Japanese shipping, 15 percent of coal and metal mining, 50 percent of flour milling, 59 percent of sheet-glass production, and (in March 1945) 16 percent of all bank assets. And Mitsubishi was small in relation to Mitsui, which, by the end of the war, had an estimated *three million* employees and 6 percent of all the capital in Japan.

Probably it was inevitable, given the American suspicion of big business that characterized the early years of the Occupation, that the *zaibatsu* would be fingered as public enemy number one by the Supreme Commander of the Allied Powers (SCAP). The acronym referred to both a person, Douglas MacArthur, and his headquarters across the moat from the Imperial Palace. In addition to repatriating and disarming several million Japanese soldiers, imposing democracy, drafting a constitution, and stripping the emperor of his divinity, SCAP set out to transform the Japanese economy into a paragon of laissez-faire capitalism.

A team of antitrust experts led by Corwin Edwards, a professor of economics from Northwestern University, was dispatched to analyze the Japanese economy. In his government report of January 1946, Edwards wrote that "Japan's industry has been under the control of a few great combines [the *zaibatsu*] supported and strengthened by the Japanese government. The concentration of control has encouraged the persistence of semifeudal relations between employer and employee, held down wages, and blocked the development of labor unions. It has discouraged the launching of independent business ventures and thereby retarded the rise of a Japanese middle class." Thus, in the spirit of egalitarianism, the family-based *zaibatsu* were shaken to pieces—their holding companies dismantled, their shares confiscated, their owner-families purged.

Surprisingly little has been written in English about the subsequent fate of the *zaibatsu*. Sometime in early 1948, with unemployment in Japan running high and the Japanese labor movement gaining strength, SCAP—prodded by American politicians and business leaders—began to fear the rise of communism in Japan. Big business was seen as an antidote. There was no explicit change in policy toward the *zaibatsu*, but many who have written about the American Occupation note a change in attitude. The fanaticism went out of the American campaign against the *zaibatsu*. Purged business leaders were permitted to return to their companies. Antimonopoly laws written by SCAP in 1947 were diluted in 1949, and, except for the statute outlawing holding companies, were virtually ignored by the Japanese government from the time SCAP withdrew in 1952.

The repairing of the damage caused by SCAP continues apace. Perhaps the most dramatic illustration of the trend away from individual sovereignty and toward corporate hegemony is in the structure of the stock market. In 1950 about 70 percent of all corporate shares were held by individuals. Today it is corporations that hold 70 percent of the shares. In the three months I was in Japan, Mitsubishi Cement merged with Mitsubishi Mining, and Taisho Marine & Fire announced its intention to change its name to Mitsui Marine & Fire. By one conservative estimate the Big Six intermarket groups, the modern *zaibatsu*, now control 15 percent of the total assets of the Japanese economy, 17 percent of the total sales, the top five commercial banks, trust banks, and insurance companies, and—most significantly for an American trying to sell corporate insurance—56 of the largest 100 manufacturing companies.

Only two of the reforms wrought during the American Occupation in the direction of laissez-faire capitalism have stuck: the removal of the families that ruled the *zaibatsu* and the dissolution of the holding companies through which the activities of various companies within the group could be closely coordinated. And on September 1, 1990, Japan's leading economic journal, the *Nihon Keizai Shimbun*, reported that one of these looked like it might be changing. For the first time since the American Occupation, the idea of reviving the holding companies was formally and publicly discussed. "Nearly the entire business community," the article stated, "has put its weight behind the politically charged move to revise the Anti-Monopoly Law, ending the prohibition against corporations forming holding companies." Since the activities of companies contained within the Big Six modern *zaibatsu* already appear well coordinated, a change in the law may be of little practical consequence. One reason given for the proposed change was that it would render existing arrangements more transparent to the foreigners who complained about hidden Japanese conspiracies. The conspiracy would then be visible.

One way to view the commercial history of postwar Japan is as a steady march by business executives back to their former glory. The economics of piling together vast numbers of unrelated businesses may be ambiguous (who in the West still speaks of synergy?), but the politics are clear: size equals bargaining power with bureaucrats, vis-à-vis smaller Japanese enterprises. The bureaucrats do not oppose the trend toward bigger business, partly because they tend to retire early and accept lucrative jobs within the cartels, and also, no doubt, because a few big companies are easier to oversee from a ministry desk than a lot of smaller ones.

"The attitude here," says Collins, "is that what's good for Tokio Marine is good for Japan." It is now an embarrassing cliché to suggest that corporate stability is more highly valued in Japan than elsewhere; but it is one of those clichés that also seems true. Stronger enforcement of antitrust laws is high on the list of demands that U.S. trade negotiators are making of Japan. But it raises an interesting question: If MacArthur couldn't eliminate the *zaibatsu* at gunpoint, how can U.S. trade representative Carla Hills do it with words? As both Collins and Cropp said, "She can't."

All this had profound consequences for Collins, who had superior wares that he could not sell, mainly because of the stranglehold of the *zaibatsu* insurers. Guaranteed market share, together with the pampering by the Ministry of Finance, has left domestic Japanese insurance companies flabby and inefficient (Japanese insurers, Collins pointed out, have always lost money when they've had to compete in foreign markets). Yet Collins was shut out. Seventy-five percent of his business in Japan was transacted with foreign companies in Japan. His conclusion: "You don't break in very well locally; what you do instead is sell to foreigners coming here."

Because of the business groups, many domestic markets are in a steady state. The market for insurance happens to include one outsider: AIU. Why? Was AIU, like innocence in the prelapsarian paradise, included in the original design? Collins shook his head when I asked him, not because he didn't want to help, but because AIU had been established as part of the system long before he arrived. "You should talk to the Captain," Collins said, as if I should know whom he meant. And soon enough, I would.

AIU Corporation followed the U.S. Army into Japan in 1946. Its American CEO, Cornelius Vander (C.V.) Starr, had a lifelong love of the Far East. He had founded his first insurance company 30 years earlier in Shanghai, and only later moved its headquarters to the States. Starr couldn't have picked a better moment to enter Japan. In 1946 insurance licenses were granted not by the Ministry of Finance but by SCAP. This was one of the temporary cracks opened by the Occupation on the surface of the

"The Captain" (Masayoshi Munakata) is keeper to the shrine of C. V. Starr, the former chairman of American International Group.

Japanese economy through which a nimble American business-man could leap. The leading Japanese insurance men had a say in what happened in their market, but as AIU president Buck Freeman, who accompanied Starr on his early trips to Japan, points out, "It would have been difficult for them to refuse us under the circumstances."

In a climate briefly friendly to newcomers, AIU began to peddle a new kind of insurance, first to American soldiers and then, in 1951, to Japanese civilians. "Starr introduced an entire country to a new concept," says Collins. Until his arrival, Japanese insurance had been distinctly inferior to its Western counterpart. The Japanese had lagged in this field for a long time. The *zaibatsu* insurers, for example, had no claims departments. Under the prevailing automobile policies, the insured negotiated his own settlement, a state of affairs especially repugnant to a people who loathe confrontation. As Freeman says, "No one wants to negotiate with a guy they just ran over." Once having decided the damages, the beleaguered insured Japanese faced a 20 percent deductible, i.e., he had to pay 20 percent of the claim out of his own pocket.

"We became popular overnight," says Freeman, "and not only with customers. People were looking for jobs, and because we had such a desirable product, it was easy for us to hire agents to sell it." By 1952 AIU had the largest share of the markets in both automobile and personal-accident insurance of any company in Japan. Starr then hired John Royceton, the head of the insurance division at SCAP headquarters, to manage his Japanese branch. Royceton had acquired a reputation among the Japanese for his leniency toward the *zaibatsu* combines; he was owed favors. "The Japanese would have done anything for Royceton," says Freeman, "short of putting up his statue in their boardrooms."

Enter the Captain. "The Captain," Collins has said, "left just before I arrived. He worked at AIU from the late 1940s. People around the office didn't call him the Captain anymore. He was known as the Enemy. You weren't supposed to talk to him. But I figured anybody whom AIG chief executive Maurice Greenberg called 'the Enemy' was worth knowing." His name, it turned out, was Masayoshi Munakata. He had spent a long career with AIU as comptroller and chief financial officer. The Captain trained tank crews for the imperial army right up until the end of World War II. When, in late 1945, the war ceased to provide employment, the Captain, along with several million other young men, began looking for a job. In 1948 he was introduced by a U.S. Army captain to one of the new American companies in Japan, AIU. He landed in the accounting department, which made sense, because in his words, "I could not speak a single word English."

The Captain would make a good guest on *What's My Line?* From a group of 20 Japanese men plucked randomly from the street, he would probably seem the least likely to have trained tank crews in the imperial army or be known to anyone as the Enemy. He is short and round-faced with eyes that blink about three times more than they should. He was, when we met, painfully polite. The imperfections in his English seemed to enhance the sentiment he wished to express, like a waiter who speaks English with a French accent. "Mistah C. V. Stah was very smart man," said the Captain. "He knew the Japanese people. He knew Eastern thinking. I devoted to AIU because of C. V. Stah."

The Captain's primary sentiment was a deep and abiding loyalty to the memory of a man dead more than 22 years. He carried with him a short biography of Starr, published after his death. "My most important book," said the Captain, pointing to its epigraph: THE SPIRIT NEVER DIES. I noticed he had underlined several lines describing Starr. "There were no nationalities or races for him . . . his imperative was people . . . his inner fire . . . his genuine admiration for the Oriental . . . the consideration Starr showed his employees was repaid in kind. . . . " The Captain turned to a photograph of Starr—tall and lean with an impossibly strong chin, a crisp bow tie, and a benevolent gaze. He looked self-conscious, as if he were personifying the American Century. "He my everything," said the Captain.

"About Mr. Stah," the Captain continued, "I remember three stories." The first was set in 1963, 15 years after he had joined AIU. The Captain was up for a promotion to director of AIU. To become a director, however, one had to pass a test of Starr's devising, which Starr traveled to Japan to administer personally. On this day in 1963, there were five candidates assembled in a conference room.

According to the Captain, "Mr. Stah said to us, 'AIU is American company. Suppose war between Japan and America happen again. American company not popular. Japanese employee not popular. How do you protect lives of Japanese family?'" It deeply impressed the Captain that Starr gave even a passing thought to the welfare of his Japanese employees. "This Stah very smart. Think of everything," said the Captain. (The answer was to make AIU a Japanese chartered company. Four of the five candidates, including the Captain, passed.)

"Second story," said the Captain, who looked as if he'd just relived the glorious moment in which he was made a director of AIU. "Stah says, 'Captain, now you director I should visit your house.' I had just bought 50-*tsubo* [more than 1,500-square-foot] house. I was very proud Mr. Stah wanted to visit house. Then Mr. Stah he came and said, 'This home too small for my director.' He said I had to have 100-*tsubo* house.

"I said to Mr. Stah, 'One-hundred-*tsubo* house very expensive.' I said, 'Mr. Stah, I don't have money.' Mr. Stah said, 'Captain, money is in bank.'

"Every day, I help the world's most stylish women get dressed."

Jeffrey Spiegel
Worldwide Account Executive, New York City

PartsBank®, the Federal Express warehousing, inventory control, and distribution service,
allows designers to bring their latest creations in from Europe, into
the finest stores, in just days. Giving retailers priceless extra days to sell them.

"This Stah is such a guy, you know," the Captain said. "That's why Japanese employee still devoted to Mr. Stah's company."

From his new 100-*tsubo* house, the Captain set about trying to fulfill what he calls Mr. Starr's mission: to obtain a license from the Ministry of Finance to sell life insurance; to erect a building of which the company could be proud; and to turn AIU into a Japanese chartered company.

Starr died in 1968, before any of the goals had been reached. So the Captain assumed personal responsibility for the mission. It was not until 1971 that AIU obtained a license to sell life insurance. Then the Captain set about trying to get a permit from the Ministry of Construction for the building of a major office.

AIU was, and is, in an unusual position for a foreign company. It owns vast tracts of land in Tokyo. Land has always been the primary unit of wealth in Japan, and Japanese part with it reluctantly. For a very brief period after the war, however, money was more important than land, and the society was briefly fluid. Fortunes and dynasties arose from the unusually high property-turnover rate after the war. While most of the nation was ruined, an unlikely handful of Japanese had access to cash or credit. To this day the source of much of that money remains a mystery; it is presumed to have come, at least in part, from Americans associated with SCAP.

Walking around Tokyo, you can see evidence of this rare moment when the status quo temporarily yielded to change. There are buildings with rounded corners in the middle of city blocks. These were designed to stand at the intersection of boulevards planned by SCAP (they were abandoned after SCAP's departure). There is a chain of hotels called Prince that sits on billions of dollars' worth of real estate. It was bought by Yasujiro Tsutsumi, who bequeathed it to his son Yoshiaki, who *Forbes* magazine estimates is the world's richest man. The Tsutsumi family company, the Seibu group, is the largest owner of unoccupied Tokyo real estate, the best of it purchased just after the war from the largest of distressed sellers, the Japanese imperial family. The Tokyo Prince Hotel was built on the former graveyard of the Tokugawas, the shoguns who closed Japan to foreigners in the mid-1600s and ruled the country until 1868. The Takanawa Prince Hotel was formerly the Tokyo mansion of Prince Takeda.

C. V. Starr had roughly the same idea as Yasujiro Tsutsumi. He knew a strapped landlord when he saw one. The head of a small *zaibatsu* called Asano owned precious land beside the Imperial Palace and needed money to pay his inheritance taxes. Starr hired a senior manager named Sakai Suzuki, who had been purged by SCAP from Tokio Marine & Fire. Suzuki negotiated in his own name for the Asano properties. Within two years of his arrival, Starr had bought 13 properties from the Asano financial group.

But that was just the start of Starr's mission. Acquiring land in Japan is easy compared with removing the people who happen to live on it. A ramshackle dormitory for the families of 15 Asano employees sat on the AIU property. Still operating in his own name, Suzuki hired a team of what one AIU employee called "very rough Japanese negotiators" to persuade the tenants to leave. After 10 years, there was only one family left inside. They occupied the top floor of the ruinous structure, which gave Suzuki an idea. He hired a contractor to lift the roof off the building and leave the family inside exposed to the elements. "This is something we never could have done under our own name," said one AIU executive. The first day it rained, the family sued for damages. Once the case reached the courts, a compromise was struck and the family moved. It was 1966.

The AIU building was now scheduled to rise on the site abutting the grounds of the Imperial Palace. But there was a rule that, because no person should look down upon the Imperial Palace, no building near it could rise more than 31 meters. By 1974 the Japanese government was willing to grant AIU an exception. The building could overlook the palace, but should never be visible to a person gazing out a window on the palace's ground floor. "We had to think about this one," says president Freeman. "And we went back to them and said, 'Yes, but how *tall* a person?' And they said, 'Oh, about the height of the emperor.'"

So two lines were drawn: one straight up from the ground owned by AIU and the other from a point 5 feet 4 inches above the floor of the Imperial Palace. Their point of intersection became the new regulation height for buildings surrounding the palace. The AIU building rose as a sort of monument to shrewd judgment and good luck. It is this building that people in Japan think of when you mention the name AIU. From the top floor there was a lovely view of the palace roof. In the lobby there was a bust of C. V. Starr. And on the tablet of the real estate assessor was a value of $2 billion.

I began to wonder how on earth the Captain, who had been so devoted, had become the Enemy. The Captain said the trouble had started four years earlier, when C.V. Starr's successor, Maurice Greenberg, began to doubt the Captain's mission. In its 71-year history, AIU has had only two chief executives—Starr and Greenberg. The Captain says Greenberg is a "business genius, but he never have Mr. Stah's heart. Mr. Stah was so-called romantic." (Albeit one who lifted the roof from people's homes.) Greenberg had wanted to sell AIU's landholdings in 1970 and was firmly against the construction of the new building. "He say, 'Captain, building is meaningless.' I say it is a symbol of the people's hard working. I say it is part of mission established by Mr. Stah, and I should follow Mr. Stah. He say, 'Where is Mr. Stah now?'"

The Captain wanted to finish the mission by turning AIU into a Japanese chartered company. Instead, in 1975, he was transferred from Tokyo to AIU's New York office. "I was put into icebox by Mr. Greenberg," he says. The end came when the Captain returned to Tokyo on business, walked into the AIU building, and noticed that the bust of C.V. Starr had been removed. "I questioned to my chauffeur, 'Where is the statue?' He say it thrown out. That day I put up my resignation papers to Mr. Freeman. He say, 'Captain, if you resign now you lose retirement benefit.' I say I know that. That's all he care about, retirement benefit."

Coldblooded American versus sentimental Japanese, Western reason versus the Japanese heart, is as recurrent a theme in Japan's commerce as it is in Japan's books and films. In the interest of drama, the Westerner is often made to seem even more ruthlessly reasonable than he truly is. Yet I had met and spoken with Freeman, and had difficulty imagining him as anything but generous. I figured I had better pay a call on AIU to see what had happened to that bust of C.V. Starr. I soon found myself in an AIU elevator, across the moat from the Imperial Palace, ascending to a point just beneath the emperor's line of vision.

"Oh, yeah," said one of the executives who greeted me as I stepped out of the elevator, "where did that thing go?"

Having failed to solve the mystery of the founder's bust, I mentioned the Captain. The room went silent. Quite clearly, he was still the Enemy. Not because he had quit, but because he had taken 30 people and about $100 million of business with him to a rival company.

The Captain is a good example of how doing business in Japan has changed as the system has steadily ossified. If he were entering the market for the first time today, it is hard to believe that even the Captain would work at a small start-up American company, when there are seven jobs with Japanese companies for every young Japanese graduate. And when I asked my AIU host if C. V. Starr could have built his company in modern-day Japan, he said probably not. It was the only sentiment of the Captain's shared by AIU's top brass. "You could *never* start now," Buck Freeman told me. "I don't think you could even find the employees."

Still, the company founded by Starr is entrenched in the Japanese marketplace. "We have learned to survive in the Japanese jungle," says Freeman, "and it *is* a jungle." AIU makes good money in Japan, benefiting as much as any Japanese company from the system of fixed prices and the exclusion of new entrants. If it doesn't expand its market share, it doesn't lose any either; and it grows with the Japanese market as a whole. AIU regularly hires officials who have retired from the Ministry of Finance. Indeed, says Bob Collins, the Ministry of Finance would probably watch out for AIU with as much concern as it would for a Japanese company, for it is as much a part of the system as any Japanese company—even if it lacks a Japanese charter. As Collins said (again forgetting he no longer works there), "We are part of the establishment—one doesn't rock the boat, does one?"

This is indicative of the general pattern of commerce in Japan. The companies best positioned to see, understand, and articulate the injustices of the system are also the least likely to speak out for fear of jeopardizing what they have. "The only leverage you have with the MOF," says Collins, "is to agree not to make a stink in exchange for a favor like, say, permission to write policies in English." Yet even he admits that to make a stink would be "penny-wise and pound-foolish." A recent study of all Western companies with operations in Japan showed that 50 percent of them had operating profit margins higher than those anywhere else in the world, some as much as 225 percent higher. They can hardly be blamed for not wanting to make waves. But where does that leave the next C. V. Starr when he arrives in Japan to start a business?

Far from being an encouragement to other Americans, a success story such as AIU's supports the most cynical view of Japan's business practices. Even the group of AIU executives with whom I spoke had few illusions about AIU's success. They expressed sympathy for the other foreign insurance companies that had arrived too late for the game in Japan. The successful firms such as AIU actually become part of the Japanese Defense. They make it possible for Japanese trade negotiators to argue that Japan really is more or less open and that those who fail to penetrate Japanese markets simply aren't trying hard enough.

BRAND-NAME DEMONS

The major weaknesses of any rhetorical defense based upon lies and half-truths is that it can be exposed. Karel van Wolferen belongs to a newly recognized school of authors making their careers writing critically about Japan. They are known in Japan as "the revisionists" or, more commonly but unfairly, as "the Japan-bashers." Like every other group in Japan that has earned formal recognition, the new intellectual enemies have been ranked in order of importance. Ask any 10 Japanese to list the top tier of Japan-bashers, and you'd receive 10 identical lists. They would include Professor Chalmers Johnson, author of *MITI and the Japanese Miracle*; Clyde Prestowitz, former U.S. trade negotiator and author of *Trading Places*; and James Fallows, writer of numerous revisionist articles on Japan. Together their works provide what seems to me to be the first clear description of the system that so frustrates the American executive.

Van Wolferen is the only one of the group who lives in Japan, and as a result he tends to stir up the most trouble. In a speech given in Tokyo, van Wolferen put the case for reassessing Japan this way: "Until very recently, when someone wanted to understand why Japan had developed such a formidable economic presence in the world, the ready-made answers his or her questions elicited would almost inevitably consist of assertions about alleged cultural peculiarities that made the Japanese do things differently. Japanese motives, it has often been said, could not be easily fathomed by the Western observer because of insufficient understanding of Japanese culture."

The revisionists have gone looking for reasons other than cultural differences for Japan's economic success, as well as for the failure of outsiders trying to do business in Japan. "Revisionist literature," claimed van Wolferen, "is concerned with political arrangements among government institutions, industrial institutions, and social institutions that create conditions for optimum economic performance." Just the sort of arrangement that, for example, drives the Japanese insurance markets.

Many Japanese in positions of influence regard the revisionists' probings as an invasion of their homeland, and their reactions are occasionally as interesting as the revisionists themselves. In May 1989 James Fallows published his most powerful revisionist article in *The Atlantic* called "Containing Japan." The title alluded to the doctrine that once ruled American policy toward the Soviet Union.

The response in Tokyo was remarkably uniform: everyone became hysterical at once. The *Yomiuri Shimbun* (circulation 10 million) ran a piece under the headline RETURN OF THE YELLOW PERIL, fabricating quotations to make Fallows appear more antagonistic than he was. "There was no turning back from that point," says Fallows. "I was yet another foreign demon demanding tremendous sacrifices from them." Yet he was demanding simply that Japan play by the same trade rules as the United States. Japanese cultural narcissism ensured that Fallows would have the chance to repeat his views over and over to excited television reporters. By the time I arrived in Japan, it was nearly impossible to hold a conversation with a member of the educated elites without hearing the dreaded name of Fallows and some distorted version of his views. Not that Fallows isn't welcome there: "Brand-name anything has a place in Japan," he says, "and I'm a brand-name demon."

Author Karel van Wolferen belongs to the school of "Japan-bashers," who write critically about the country's economic system.

The views Fallows expressed didn't require distortion to be sensationalized. Fallows started by pointing out that Japan has defied the expectations of many economists by sustaining its trade surpluses in spite of a strengthening yen, and he went on to say that the systematic abuse by Japan of the free trading system posed a threat to American interests. The Japanese system of favoring the interests of producers over consumers, he argued, was designed to generate huge trade surpluses. The Japanese viewed trade as war, surplus as victory. In 1987, when the yen was rising against the dollar and Japanese exporters were feeling badly squeezed, a Japanese newspaper published a column that compared the foreign-exchange markets to the Pacific War. As Fallows quoted:

In a few months the yen soared from 245 to 200. This was the equivalent of Japan's loss of four aircraft carriers at Midway. . . . Washington's final objective is probably an exchange rate of ¥100 to $1. That represents Japan's total defeat and General Douglas MacArthur's triumphant entry into Tokyo. . . . We must not lose the Pacific War twice.

The consequence of this wartime mentality, said Fallows, was an abysmally low standard of living: "The same country that has the biggest cash surpluses and the largest overseas investments in the world also has by far the highest consumer prices, the highest proportion of unpaved roads among developed countries, the lowest per capita endowment of parks, sporting areas, and other public facilities, and across the board the least materially bountiful life." He then argued that because the Japanese system was effectively governed by the producers, it was unlikely to change without a shock from outside. "The significance of this system," he wrote, "is not that it is collusive—it's the opposite of centrally coordinated—but that it is stifling. The economy is broken up into tribes, and each tribe does everything possible to prevent 'confusion' in the market it regulates—confusion being a euphemism for real competition that would put inefficient producers out of business, offer new services, and lower prices. Only the skill and discipline of the Japanese work force in general keeps the whole system from breaking down." The whole of the argument led to the conclusion that the only way to deal with Japan was to impose trade sanctions.

In Tokyo last year, one heard a certain defensiveness whenever the conversation drifted—or was dragged—onto the subject of James Fallows. Early in my stay I interviewed the editor of the *Asahi Shimbun*, widely regarded as the most liberal and iconoclastic of Japan's major daily newspapers. The year before, the star political reporter at the *Asahi* had broken the scandal involving Recruit Cosmos, Japan's largest employment agency. The head of Recruit had sold shares in his company at less than their market value to virtually every powerful figure in the ruling Liberal Democratic Party as well as to a few senior Japanese business executives. The reporting of the *Asahi Shimbun* had forced the resignation of Prime Minister Takeshita. I wondered if the Japanese equivalent of Bob Woodward and Carl Bernstein had been as well compensated for his efforts (with fat book contracts, film deals, and promotions) as Woodward and Bernstein had been after Watergate. I then asked what I thought was an innocuous question: "Has Japan's Bob Woodward become rich and famous?"

The Japanese editor looked at me with a blend of scorn and pity. "That's the problem with Americans," he said.

Oh, no, I thought and looked around for a bomb shelter. "Look, forget I ever men—" I started to say.

"You Americans," he interrupted. "All you care about is short term. You only do things for promotion and money. You have to have things right now, right *now!*"

He went on at length about the decadence of any culture that could produce drug addicts, illiterates, Pete Rose, and Leona Helmsley. He had in his head a pretty complete list of ugly Americans, and I found it hard to disagree with some of his harsh judgments. He said that for a Japanese investigative reporter, the esteem of one's colleagues is payment enough. (I later spoke with Japan's Bob Woodward himself, Hiroshi Yamamoto, who agreed and claimed not to have sold movie rights.)

James Fallows, Washington, D.C., editor of *The Atlantic*, is a "brand-name demon" in Japan.

Then the Japanese editor made a strange mental jump. The Americans who wrote books and articles critical of Japan, he said, were fools. The trade deficit was entirely a matter of American businessmen's not trying hard enough. "When I read the articles by James Fallows in *The Atlantic*, I laugh there is so much wrong in them—hahahahahahaha."

I sat dumbly and listened as the Japanese editor became slightly mad. "Hahahahahaha," he continued. Finally he seemed to remember I was present. "You are not like James Fallows," he said. "You are very intelligent, I think."

It occurred to me then that the revisionists might one day be classified with Commodore Perry and General MacArthur. They have become the third wave, and the first serious intellectual assault upon the Japanese way of organizing themselves. Though (for the first time) the invasion of Japan by Americans is intellectual rather than physical, the consequences for Japanese-American relations could be equally profound.

The Japanese Defense disarms the intellectual assault by forcing the revisionists into a bottle labeled JAPAN-BASHERS. As van Wolferen has said, "The concept of Japan-bashing has made it all but impossible to discuss revisionist theories seriously. The entry of the term into conversations, news reports, editorials, and practically every Japanese article about the subject has been one of

the most pernicious developments in Japan-U.S. relations." Use
of the phrase, he said, "appears to vindicate deep-seated Japanese
apprehensions that the world, and especially the United States, is
really against Japan."

He might have added that it also diverts attention from the
original debate.

IS MAX DANGER REALLY AGAINST
THE JAPANESE?

One of the first observations made by the American visitor to
Tokyo is how often, for a place with a population of 11.6 million,
he bumps into other Westerners. That is because Western executives in Japan, in a search for familiar comforts, squeeze into
Roppongi, the Western quarter of Tokyo. (I met one American
housewife who bragged that she hadn't spoken to a Japanese for
six months.) This no doubt suits a lot of Japanese. When IBM
moved 200 families to Japan in 1984, Japanese newspapers ran
features comparing them to the arrival of the black ships of
Matthew Perry, as if a few American executives were going to
change Japan.

Their concerns were misplaced. Tossing a few more barbar-
ians into Roppongi (the modern cage?) wasn't likely to affect
conditions outside. Roppongi contains the American Embassy,
the American Chamber of Commerce, the Hotel Okura—lodg-
ing of choice for American businessmen and U.S. trade negotiators—a dozen or so *Homats* (Western-style apartment
buildings), and the soul of the American community: the Tokyo
American Club. Once on the grounds of the American Club,
you might as well be in Greenwich, Connecticut. The only
traces of Japan are on the bar walls, where there hang soft-porn
Orientalist wood-block prints created in Minnesota by a man
named Cliff.

The main difference between the American Club and an
American country club is that the American Club has more of
everything: 10 bowling lanes, day-care centers, play-group areas,
a bookstore, barber and beauty shops, saunas, weight rooms,
aerobics classes, a basketball court, three paddle-tennis courts, an
Olympic-size swimming pool, a video library with 30,000
tapes, a ballroom for 500, a movie theater, suites of private
rooms, card rooms, a bakery, a butcher shop, a laundry, and so

"Provides immediate relief from stress and anxiety."

Kelvin Dorch
Courier, Toronto, Canada

From pick-up to delivery, we can tell you within seconds exactly where on
Earth your shipment is. That's because, from the moment we receive it, your shipment is
entered into our worldwide tracking network with this SuperTracker® scanner, the
only device of its kind in the industry. It may be small, but it can take a big load off your mind.

Bob Collins at his last board meeting as president of the Tokyo American Club: "I'm looking forward to heckling the next big cheese."

many restaurants that the club's manager couldn't give the exact number off the top of his head.

This cornucopia of pleasure, coupled with the difficulty of making oneself comfortable in a foreign culture, encourages American businessmen in Tokyo to pass a meaningful amount of their time at the club, pretending they are back home. It surprised no one, except perhaps a few Japanese newspapermen, when the 200 families sent to Japan by IBM, having settled into Western-style apartments, quickly became devoted members of the American Club and disappeared from the streets. "Love it or hate it, it's the center of expatriate life in Japan," says Bob Collins, who for six years served as club president.

In the hothouse social world of the expatriate, Collins is best known as the author of a column in a local English-language newspaper, *The Tokyo Weekender*, in which he fictionalizes what he sees and hears at the American Club. "Max Danger: The Adventures of an Expat in Tokyo" describes the everyday life of an American businessman and supports the widely held view that almost everything that happens to an American in Japan is based upon some misunderstanding. Max Danger has Nipples Akimbo, a Japanese secretary with unpredictable passions, and a Japanese golfing partner named Serious Hirose who is always fainting on the fairways. Max works in an intelligent office building that suffers nervous breakdowns. Almost everything bad that can happen to an executive has happened to Max, and once you've read a dozen or so episodes you begin to understand the relief on the faces of people entering the disaster-free zone of the American Club.

It seemed impossible to go more than a few days without having something happen that belonged in a Max Danger book, i.e., experiencing firsthand the defenses of a society built without the idea that outsiders might want to simply visit. Long before I found Bob Collins, I found myself in trouble. A friendly Japanese publisher had insisted upon showing me a genuine Japanese businessman's night on the town. We had just finished a boozy dinner, and he was paying the bill with his business card (the business cards of large firms double as charge cards; the bills are sent to the companies, which subsidize such binges), when he extended an invitation. "It would be an honor," he slurred to our translator, "if Michael-san would accompany me to a Ginza hostess bar."

Japanese executives are far more serious about hostesses than Americans are about hookers. A few years back, a book called *A Textbook for Nightlife* hit Japanese bestseller lists. It was treated by the local businessmen with the same plodding earnestness with which American businessmen greeted Dale Carnegie's *How to Win Friends and Influence People* in the 1950s and 1960s. The textbook outlined for the young and rising Japanese executive the rules of behavior in the company of a bar hostess. For example:

> Everybody resembles someone else. This is particularly true of hostesses who use the same makeup techniques as actors and entertainers. Now, when you meet a hostess for the first time, you don't just blurt out that she looks like a certain famous singer. Everybody does that. What you do is talk about the singer in the most glowing terms, how sexy she is, and so on. Then as nonchalantly as you can, you let it slip how much your hostess resembles the singer.

Having scanned the textbook, I was aware of the potential complications ahead. I was relieved, as we entered the hostess bar, by its familiar feel. A piece of reproduction furniture here, an imitation Monet there. Plump stuffed chairs like Grandma used to have. I was the only foreigner in sight and could sense everyone working hard not to stare.

Our party of three was ushered to a table in a corner and instantly attended by five young ladies: Kiko, Miko, Yuko, and a couple of others with equally improbable names. They wore Mickey Mouse watches. They spoke in voices an octave higher than the average birdsong. I would not have been surprised to learn that they slept with stuffed animals. Kiko, distinguished by a sizable gap between her teeth and her ability to giggle in English, poured whiskey and water into our glasses and served cheese balls and fruit. She was the talker. "Tee-hee," she said.

At last she made way for an attractive older woman who was in her early forties but claimed to be 34 and wore a funny pin through her hair. She was the owner of the bar, and looked about as professional as a person can who shuffles around in a kimono. We exchanged business cards, and then the Mama-san, as she was called, conducted the orchestra of praise and flattery that Kiko and the other Disney characters showered upon my Japanese host. He took it in for a few minutes, like a cat having his neck scratched. Occasionally he replied with—judging from the giggles he elicited—praise on the order of "You have the lips of Kathleen Turner and the feet of Susan Sarandon."

Then, without warning, he turned sniffy. He spat out a few curt Japanese words that my translator declined to interpret but that I later learned were "Please don't bother too much with me. Make the foreigner happy. He's a very rich American writer." The Mama-san and her charges shifted around in unison and looked for the first time at me. I felt inadequate, like an empty bank vault.

"Is he married?" asked the Mama-san.

"No," said the publisher.

It didn't matter that it wasn't true (I am married, and I hadn't seen a dime of royalties from my recently published book). All of a sudden a tiny, soft hand fluttered like a dove onto my knee, and Kiko was saying, "I like American men best because they are strong and know how to tell a joke." By the end of the evening we had sworn eternal friendship, and I had agreed to return the next night as the Mama-san's honored guest. Alone.

"A great honor," said a stuffy old Englishman I had met early in my stay in Tokyo. He had lived for years with the vain belief that he knew everything there was to know about the local culture. Tokyo is full of such elderly frauds, who in my brief experience were invariably graduates of British public schools. They spend their time peddling bad advice to newcomers like me, who know even less than they do.

"But can I afford this honor?" I asked, knowing that nights in the Ginza could easily run to thousands of dollars, and having nobody but the old Englishman to ask.

"Oh, you would never be expected to pay. Money is never discussed in the Ginza hostess bars," said this very great expert on Japan. He chuckled at my naiveté and crass materialism. "You needn't even carry your wallet."

The Mama-san had lured me back by promising to tell me all she knew from her years of observing Japanese businessmen: how they held their liquor, what they said about American cars—that sort of thing. She never told me anything, of course. The Mama-san treated information as if it were money. She was a shrewd titan of commerce. She was saving for the day when the yen would be strong against the dollar. She was in the market for property in Cape Cod, where she had heard there were distressed sellers. She had a friend, a noodle-shop owner, who leased Boeing 747s as a tax shelter, and she was considering the loophole herself. She thought American women weak because they "don't control the family money." She asked what I thought of the Japanese stock market. She felt it was overvalued (and she was right: it fell by 50 percent in the following six months). She spoke about six words of English, but she spoke them well.

The first of these words was *Amex*. This was her favorite word. She spoke it often, and each time she did she made a little square in the air with her fingers: the sign of the card. After the last drink in her establishment, she first raised the question of payment: "Amex?" She said it in a high-pitched chirp that I took to be her bid to seem soft and vulnerable. Later, as we staggered through a night on the town, it became a command: "Amex!" It boomed like a volley from a cannon. When I retired to my hotel in the heart of Tokyo at 4:30 a.m., I had consumed exactly two glasses of weak whiskey and was billed $575 on my American Express card. My hostess, Cape Cod landlady and stock-market speculator, had traveled for free—and turned a tidy profit for her establishment in the bargain. Her final words to me were translated, "Michael-san, you are very American."

When I told this tale to Bob Collins as he drove me home after one of our meetings, I could see him wondering whether to send Max into a hostess bar in his next column. We passed through Kasumigaseki, home to the various ministries that oversee Japanese business and finance with which Collins so often tangles.

"Young Mister Lewis!" he said, grinding the gears of his car into second. "A sucker is born every minute in America, and half of them find their way to Japan."

It wasn't, he explained, that I was taken for a ride. It's just that there is no such concept as a nonpaying guest in the Ginza. And by the way, it probably didn't help that I had such an *American* way about me. "My approach when I first got here," he said, "was to be straightforward and direct. *Refreshingly* straightforward and direct. I thought I was very refreshing. People would say to me, 'Ahhhh, Collins-san, you are very American.' And I thought it was a compliment!"

Collins paused for a moment. "But tell me," he said. "Did she make any improper advances?"

"She told me she loved me," I said. Which was true. These were among the final words of English the Mama-san spoke to me immediately before her last request for my credit card. Whereupon the lady with the gap in her teeth had leaned over to me and whispered, "The Mama-san always says to us that love is money." Looking back, I see I may have mistaken the Mama-san. She may not have been saying "I love you," but "I love you, Amex!"

CHAPTER 4

JAPANESE OFFENSE

How courteous is the Japanese
He always says, "Excuse it, please,"
He climbs into his neighbor's garden
And smiles, and says, "I beg your pardon."
He bows and grins a friendly grin,
And calls his hungry family in;
He grins and bows a friendly bow;
"So sorry, this my garden now."
                              —Ogden Nash

Two hundred and fifty miles south of Tokyo, or three hours by bullet train, lies Japan's second city, Osaka. I journeyed there to meet Shuji Tomikawa, the 31-year-old New York representative of Mitsui Real Estate. Shuji is unusual among Japanese businessmen. He is open, talkative, engaging, almost embarrassingly blunt, and happy to drag along an American journalist wherever he goes. He had flown back to Japan to sell a Manhattan skyscraper newly erected on Fifth Avenue across from the New York Public Library. Mitsui had been holding the property for nearly two years. Now, with the New York property market collapsing, Mitsui had decided it would prefer that someone else enjoy the pleasures of ownership. The price tag was about $100 million. There was no point in looking around America for a buyer; nearly everyone in America wanted to sell. The young Japanese executive looking to make a name for himself had only one place to go.

The potential buyer was a Japanese man in his early thirties whom I'll call Beauregard (Shuji asked that he be disguised). Like many young Japanese millionaires, Beauregard had inherited his father's businesses—once a chain of inns and now a chain of parking garages. The theme common to both inns and parking

Shuji Tomikawa acquired a taste for the Brooks Brothers power look at Harvard, but he removes his suspenders before receiving Japanese guests for fear of appearing too American.

lots was land without tenants. The main parking lots in Beauregard's portfolio sat squarely on a couple of mouthwatering acres in midtown Osaka. Osaka real estate values had nearly doubled in 1989 and were now, in June 1990, about 90 percent of the legendary values of downtown Tokyo, where a square foot could cost $40,000. Beauregard's main lot had been appraised at about $600 million, and any Japanese bank would be willing—*willing?* delighted!—to lend Beauregard $600 million to spend as he pleased. So it was propitious that, like a lot of family businesses in Japan, Beauregard Enterprises had recently diversified into real estate speculation.

Beauregard was just one of many Japanese who had discovered the joy of using other people's money. Shuji said there were probably several thousand small Osaka landlords who could and would persuade a bank to lend them the money to buy the Mitsui building. Japanese banks and finance companies had been hungry to lend for the last few years (although in the last months of 1990 that changed, and by edict of the Ministry of Finance, money is no longer available for real estate speculation). Loans provided by Japan's giant city banks had been running at about 30 percent of GNP through the postwar years and right up until 1983, when all of a sudden they rose to 50 percent of GNP. The city banks alone had financed about $300 billion of land purchases, much of it purely speculative. Like South Sea Company shares in 18th-century England and tulip bulbs in 17th-century Holland, in late-20th-century Japan land had become the object of a speculative mania—all thanks to the banks.

By June of 1989, the Japanese banking system was a giant, teetering pyramid—an upside-down one, at that—kept standing only by rising property prices. The Ministry of Finance was trying to dismantle the pyramid brick by brick without causing a general collapse. The banks, for their part, could not stop making real estate loans without precipitating a crash. A lovely little exhibit of modern Japanese business practice—a small Osaka trading company called Itoman & Company, which had newly acquired landholdings of 1.2 trillion yen ($8 billion)—was located just around the corner from Beauregard's main parking lot. To buy the land, Itoman had borrowed 1.2 trillion yen from Sumitomo Bank, a transaction facilitated by the presence of a former Sumitomo banker at the helm of Itoman. Now, with real estate markets around the world looking shaky, Sumitomo wanted its money back. At the same time, the bank, seeing no contradiction, was attempting to lend Beauregard the money to buy land in America. The Japanese Offense—a term I'll use to describe the pattern of Japanese commerce overseas—was perhaps less straightforward than it appeared.

Earlier, Shuji and I had walked around the $600 million garage. Until recently, Shuji's family had owned a chain of bathhouses in Tokyo; the chain too has been parlayed into a real estate company. Shuji knows the value of Japanese land, and when he saw this particular piece, he just shook his head and smiled. "That," he whispered to me, "is worth a *lot* of money." I looked the place up and down. It was really only a big tin shed, badly in need of paint. There didn't even seem to be very many cars parked inside. Even though the Japanese property market operates by different rules than its American counterpart (first rule of thumb: in the former the land is worth eight times the building, while in the latter the building is worth eight times the land), an assessment of $600 million seemed extreme. I stared at the shed and tried mouthing a few times the words *six hundred million dollars.*

"Don't do that," said Shuji.

"Do what?" I asked.

"Stare," he replied.

I didn't see the harm in it. I mean, as far as anyone could tell we were just two guys passing by on the sidewalk in the middle of a sunny Osaka weekday. But I noticed that Shuji was walking with his head down, pretending not to look.

"You look like a spy," I said.

He shot me another vaguely annoyed look and, once we were out of lip-reading range, said, "It is rude to stare at someone else's property!"

Every day in Japan one learns of another fine rule in an elaborate code of etiquette. You can stare at wives but not at parking lots. The parking-lot attendants, Shuji explained, had probably all been warned that the man from Mitsui's New York office was in town to talk about a property deal. Shuji feared that if they saw him staring at the parking lot they would think he was scheming to buy it out from under them. "Maybe," said Shuji, "the workers run and tell Beauregard that Mitsui was staring at his property."

As we rounded the corner, we caught a glimpse of Beauregard's office, a shack behind the tin shed. It had one small window and even less paint on it than the shed. I imagined Beauregard inside stacking and restacking his gold coins like a Japanese Scrooge. Shuji had his own thought. "That's one difference between America and Japan," he said. "American businessmen call themselves professional because they have a big office and a secretary. Here people are making $1 million and they can't even find space to talk on the phone."

An hour later I watched Shuji, seated at a table in the cocktail lounge of the Nikko Hotel, attempt to sell to the owner of the tin shed the Mitsui skyscraper across from the New York Public

Library. I was kept at a safe distance by two young local businessmen. One (call him Irv) was a 34-year-old real estate agent. He wore a paisley tie and matching handkerchief. There was about him, in the context of Japanese austerity, a whiff of decadence. His eyes wandered, as if a better deal might walk though the door at any moment. I was told that he made millions of dollars each year from his family's real estate agency, about half of which he reported on the family's tax returns. The rest was what the Japanese call black money, which is paid in cash and never again mentioned. With such cash he had bought his Jaguar, his Mercedes, and his BMW. Irv had introduced Shuji to Beauregard, and, if the sale went through, stood to earn a million dollars. In America he would have been thought a success. In Japan he was merely disreputable.

The second young man (call him Homer) was both a leader in Osaka's commercial circles and an old friend of Shuji's. He had introduced Shuji to Irv. Without this web of connections, Homer explained, Shuji Tomikawa would have gone nowhere in Osaka, since Shuji worked for Mitsui and Osaka was Sumitomo's turf. Homer had just taken over *his* family company, an auto-parts manufacturer on the fringe of Osaka. Although his balance sheet revealed he was worth almost $45 million, and he had his own chunks of Osaka land up his sleeve, he felt poor as he sat in the midst of even greater local real estate fortunes. He pointed at Irv, who sat smoking beside him. "He gets to work at 11:30 each morning and leaves by four in the afternoon," said Homer, "and he makes many millions of dollars each year." He let that sink in. "Sometimes," he added, "I wonder what I'm doing making *things*." As the Japanese manufacturer of auto parts grew disconsolate watching the son of the owner of a chain of bathhouses and the son of the owner of a chain of parking lots decide whether to borrow $100 million to buy a Manhattan skyscraper, I thought for the first time that decadence in Japan might stand half a chance.

Peering over this wall of millionaires, I was able to see the business being done. It was strikingly informal. A week before, Shuji had traveled to Osaka to pitch another Mitsui building to yet another Osaka millionaire. He had carried with him only an aerial photograph of Manhattan. He walked into his lunch meeting, pulled this crumpled piece of paper from his breast pocket, thrust it before the customer, and drew a red circle around a black dot in midtown. The client almost bought the building then and there. This time, however, Shuji had assembled a fat book about the Mitsui building, with photos, charts showing rates of return, a list of the tenants (Mitsui Mining and Smelting, the Wyatt Company, the State Bank of Australia, and a few others), and some complicated-looking financial analyses. But neither Shuji nor Beauregard seemed interested in any of the printed matter. They huddled so that their heads nearly touched.

The deal itself was fairly straightforward. Beauregard would borrow money from a Japanese bank against his previously unmortgaged $600 million tin shed. He would hand over $100 million of this borrowed money to Mitsui in exchange for 461 Fifth Avenue. The building on Fifth Avenue was designed to operate at a loss for the first five years to reduce Beauregard's tax bill in Japan. For a fee, Mitsui would continue to manage the New York property and ensure that it lost all the money promised. The intentional loss of money jars the minds of all but real estate dealers. The calculated loss of money to minimize taxes paid to governments is one of the two main threads in the logic of the property business. The other is capital. "The bottom line in real estate," says Shuji, "is that the people who have money win."

One hour and seven minutes later, Beauregard had tentatively agreed to buy a Manhattan skyscraper he had never before seen. He hadn't even glanced at the book of numbers and pictures. "He said he can't read English," said Shuji. "He looks at your eyes. Only your eyes. If he looks at the book, that's just a polite way of saying no." So much for the stereotype of the foot-dragging, document-obsessed Japanese businessman. The final decision would be made upon Beauregard's next visit to America the following week. Since he spoke no English, Shuji would escort him.

COMING TO AMERICA

Many of the 50,000 or so Japanese living and working in New York converge each weekend on Edgewater, New Jersey. The first Japanese shopping mall, the Yohan Plaza, opened there on eight acres of land in September 1988. Shuji, his wife, Yuki, their 6-month-old daughter, and I had spent an hour buying bags of food. As we drove back toward Manhattan with a trunkload of various raw items, Shuji explained how different his daily habits were from those of the typical Japanese in New York. He lived in Manhattan instead of the usual Japanese outposts in Westchester County. He hadn't joined the Nippon Club, the midtown social retreat for senior Japanese executives. He had little to do with the Japanese school. He didn't golf. He spent his free time with Americans. He had learned to honk and curse when he drove, just like a New Yorker. His wife wasn't clamoring to go home. Yuki preferred New York to Tokyo and was settling in for the duration, broadening her English vocabulary by watching *Saturday Night Live* and *Late Night With David Letterman*.

Still, most of Shuji's waking life revolved around the offices of Mitsui Real Estate on the 11th floor of the Exxon Building in New York City. If from Bob Collins's office Japan looked like an obstacle course filled with rules and bureaucrats, America, from Shuji's office, looked like a cluttered auction house. With the various financial crises generating bankrupt properties more quickly than ever, America—for those with cash—was a land of opportunity. "We don't even need the S&L crisis," said Shuji. "There are properties for sale everywhere in America." He pointed up through the sunroof of his car at a building once owned by the Marcos family and now being peddled by their former bankers.

Herein lies one of the joys of being a Japanese in America. Because distressed sellers believe that Japanese have money to burn, Japanese buyers are extremely well informed about every property before it goes onto the block. Shuji knew about the Marcos building because the Marcoses' bankers had called him to ask for Mitsui's help. As one of Shuji's American colleagues at Mitsui said, "Every major deal in the American real estate market comes across our desk."

Shuji's business card describes him as a Mitsui vice-president, but I never heard him introduced or referred to as anything other than Mitsui's New York representative. As such, his job was broken down neatly into three parts. On the rare occasions Mitsui built to sell, as with the Fifth Avenue skyscraper, he was in charge of making the sale. This meant flying back to Japan, where the big buyers lived. On the more frequent occasions when Mitsui built or bought office buildings or condominiums for its long-term real estate portfolio, as part of its drive to acquire about $3 billion more of property outside Japan, Shuji helped to locate the properties. Mitsui had just bought 200 acres in upstate New York to build a golf course for business friends of

Mitsui. Shuji was also trying to purchase land on the Upper East Side to build $75 million worth of condominiums. He had purchased a car with a sunroof, he said, so that "I can see what I might want to buy while I drive."

But it was Shuji's third role that intrigued me most: to act as cultural interpreter between Japan and America. He seemed born for the part. In the early 1950s, his uncle lived in America and sent postcards home to Japan. Shuji grew up longing to visit the land of tall buildings and open spaces, surrounded by American popular culture. His favorite toy was his G.I. Joe. He watched television shows called *New York Papa* (*Peyton Place*), *Wife Is a Witch* (*Bewitched*), and *Shrew Millionaire Family* (*The Beverly Hillbillies*). Between high school and college, he spent a year with a farming family in upstate New York. ("It was really *Little House on the Prairie*," he says. "They'd start talking about Mary, about how Mary was sick. I thought Mary was their daughter. Mary was a cow.") In college he studied American economic history and wrote his thesis on the economic advancement of black Americans after the Civil War.

After college and two years of assembling property in Tokyo on which Mitsui built apartment buildings, Shuji became the first employee of Mitsui Real Estate ever to attend Harvard Business School. The summer between his first and second years of business school, he worked in the real estate division of Goldman, Sachs, where he acquired a taste for the Brooks Brothers power look. Many large Japanese companies systematically enroll their employees in American business schools. The schools acclimate the young Japanese to America and serve to rank the graduates within a Japanese company. If you tell Shuji where a Mitsubishi executive went to business school, for example, he can tell you exactly where that executive stands in his peer group and exactly what his chances are of one day running the company. (The Japanese grade American business schools even more ruthlessly than do the most credential-crazed Americans. Only the first tier of young employees at Japan's leading international corporations are allowed to apply to Harvard, the second to Stanford, the third to Columbia, the fourth to Wharton, and so on into academic purgatory.)

In the role of cultural interpreter, Shuji escorts visiting Mitsui executives, clients, and friendly politicians who come to tour the United States. Summer is high season, and he was on call when I

arrived in New York. Mitsui was seeking the approval of officials from Fukuoka, a southern Japanese prefecture, for a waterfront development there. The officials had told Mitsui that before
they would sign off on the development they might like to see
America. So one Saturday in July, I rode with Shuji in a limousine to collect from Kennedy Airport Mitsui Real Estate's latest
guests, a group of Fukuokan bureaucrats.

While we waited for the plane to arrive from Tokyo, Shuji
handed me a copy of the itinerary. Its purpose was fuzzy. The
visitors had no plans to study American waterfront developments. They had no plans to study anything. The group of five
would arrive from Tokyo at midday, check into the Plaza Hotel,
then immediately start the tour. They would return to their hotel
late the same night, arise early the next morning, tour some
more, then hop a plane to Chicago. Less than 24 hours after
arriving in Chicago, they would fly to Orlando. Less than 24
hours after arriving in Orlando, they would fly to San Antonio.
They would continue apace through San Diego, San Francisco,
and Honolulu. Six days after they had gotten on the bus in
Fukuoka, they would land in Tokyo to a martyr's reception.
"Their wives," said Shuji, "will greet them and sympathize with
their hard travels."

"It looks more like an endurance contest than a business trip,"
I said.

Shuji laughed. "Well . . . ah yes . . . it *is*." He craned his neck
distractedly in the arrival lounge as we waited for the jumbo jet
from Narita to unload.

"Why bother?" I asked.

He stopped his craning and looked at me with a new respect.
"*Very* good question," he said. "*Very* difficult question to answer. . . . The idea is that they will be more motivated. Most of
these trips are made to incentivize the people to do a good job.
Once they get back to Fukuoka, the approval process will go
very smoothly. They will remember limousine and say, 'Gosh,
that was my perk!'"

"Yes," I said, "but what do they think they're going to
accomplish?"

"Maybe they don't even know," he said.

"Then why all the rushing around?" I asked.

"The Japanese are always like that when they are on vacation,"
he said. "They have to see everything. They want to see all the

"I'm here to answer your questions around the clocks."

Mary Lucus-Fisher
Senior Customer Service Agent, Sacramento

Whatever you need to know—from prices, packaging tips and customs regulations to the status of your shipment, pick-up to delivery—our Customer Service Centers can tell you, quickly and courteously. Twenty-four hours a day.

famous buildings."

With that, it was clear, I was supposed to be satisfied, and I was. It was apparent that the tour had nothing to do with pleasure. It had even less to do with business. It lived in the limbo of ritual reserved for Japanese tour groups. It existed for the purpose of making an impression back in Japan. In Fukuokan bureaucratic circles, said Shuji, a trip to America confers a certain amount of prestige. Not wealth, not promotion, but prestige. Prestige and status were among the goals of the Japanese Offense.

The airport lounge where Shuji and I were waiting was crowded with hundreds of Japanese. As the passengers disembarked from the plane, Shuji would describe the status of each Japanese as he cleared customs. A man passed us pulling a luggage cart. He had silver in his teeth and wore a blazer, a white polo shirt, flannel slacks, and tassel loafers. "Big fish," said Shuji. "How do you know?" I asked. "Soft luggage, soft shoes," said Shuji. "And the way he walks." Sure enough, two middle-aged executives came rushing out of the crowd to relieve the big fish of his baggage cart, as if the burden of the thing was too much for one man to bear. The big fish bowed slightly. The two medium-sized fish, in return, nearly touched their foreheads to their tail fins. Shuji shook his head and smiled. "*Very* big fish. Big guys like that carry like $20,000 on them."

I was left to ponder this little display of virtuosity while Shuji scanned the swelling mob. There is a body of Japanese literature called the *nihonjinron*, or the "theorizing on the Japanese." Buried in the ragbag of bizarre notions about what makes Japanese people unique—odd-shaped brains, delicate stomachs incapable of digesting foreign beef, etc.—is the sometimes convincing one that Japanese, more than any other people, are able to communicate without words. In a nation as highly stratified as Japan, because of the constant need to know one's position, there exist all sorts of nonverbal signs and symbols that are absent from a less hierarchical society. (It would probably have been easy to spot the big fish in feudal Europe, too.)

Shuji had never before met anyone in the arriving group. How would he identify them, short of raising a sign that read FUKUOKA ENDURANCE PLAYERS? "Easy," he said (I should have known). "This is their first time out of Japan, so they will all stick together. They will wear polo shirts and golf jackets and golfing slacks and tennis shoes. And their luggage will be *very* big plastic cases with wheels."

As if on cue, the doors from the customs area parted and out walked five Japanese men who could easily have been strolling down a fairway had they not been wheeling behind them five enormous plastic cases. They wore polo shirts, windbreakers, and sneakers. A sixth man, a representative from Mitsui's office in Fukuoka, chased behind them. Shuji apparently had been expecting him, too. "He's younger than me," Shuji realized with delight. "That's very useful. I'm going to treat him like a slave."

Riding in from the airport, I began to understand the power of Shuji's position. Shuji was Mitsui's point man, and Mitsui was the sluice through which a meaningful tonnage of Japanese businessmen passed into America. About once a week for the next four years Shuji would hire a limousine, ride to Kennedy Airport, and collect some visiting bigwig. More often than not, the visiting Japanese was completely reliant upon Shuji for his information about America; more often than not the visiting Japanese had a great deal of influence over money that would be invested in America. The Fukuoka Endurance Players, as it happened, did not. Still, in watching Shuji give his tour, I couldn't help but feel I was watching the future of Japanese investment in America being determined.

Seated in the rear of the silver stretch limousine, Shuji pulled out his map of Manhattan. It wasn't one of those paper gas-station jobs you pick up when lost in the middle of nowhere, but a three-foot-high billboard made of some poisonous kind of plastic. In the course of his stay in New York, Shuji would eventually show the same map to perhaps a thousand other visiting and equally ignorant Japanese, including his superiors at Mitsui. On the map he had highlighted in pink what he perceived to be the prime areas of Manhattan, and in blue what he felt were the next best. Everything else—perhaps 95 percent of Manhattan—was left white and ignored. It should have been titled "The Japanese View of New York." There was more than a little subjectivity involved in the coloring. The cluster of brownstones around Central Park West and 77th had been left white because they happened to contain Shuji's apartment. Shuji didn't want his superiors to think he lived too well. The badly used neighborhood around Third Avenue and 79th, an honest blue, was colored pink because it happened to contain Shuji's pet condominium project. Shuji just smiled when I asked if he ever considered the effect that these strokes of his pen might be having on Manhattan property values.

The map was a kind of Michelin guide for money. Japanese money travels like Japanese tourists: once the destination is agreed upon, it arrives in busloads. Honolulu, Los Angeles, and now New York have become the star sites for major Japanese real estate investments—the pink cities on the map of America. Shuji says the concentration occurs because Japanese people are not sophisticated, and that New York used to be the only city east of the Rocky Mountains where Japan Air Lines flies. He isn't inclined to fight the myopia. "Japanese only care about New York," he says. "Atlanta, Chicago, Detroit, Memphis. People don't care about these cities. They are same to me except some of them have different weather." Read "they would all be white on the Japanese map of America." An economist would say that as the prices in pink Manhattan rise, the returns will fall—as they have already—and that natural economic laws will redirect Japanese investment toward Indiana or some such place. Shuji isn't so sure. "The opportunity might be better," says Shuji, "and it might be more profitable, but it would take 10 years for me to persuade Tokyo to build condominiums in Indiana."

The group from Fukuoka acquired a second limousine for the ride into the city. As we pulled away from the airport and onto the highway, the limousine in which I rode filled with cigarette smoke, and the characters of the two men from Fukuoka began to emerge. One of them wore a black belt with NCAA stenciled around it in white letters. He wanted more than anything to sleep, and his head bounced against the windowpane to the vibration of the potholes in the highway. The other was chubby and bossy: the senior administrator. He announced after a few minutes that he was unfazed by jet lag and that the tour of New York should proceed as soon as possible. This pronouncement was superfluous, since Shuji intended to run him and his fellow government inspectors into the ground. But it did contribute to the mood of urgency.

The Japanese stared out the windows at America. Shuji pointed at the Manhattan skyline, then to a lone skyscraper recently erected in Queens by Citicorp. It rose from a cluster of ancient warehouses beside the highway as if it had been dropped carelessly by the giant that had created the city of towers in the distance. Shuji explained that Citicorp had just sold a majority stake in its flagship building on 53rd and Lexington to a subsidiary of Dai-Ichi Mutual Life Insurance. They were left with this oddly placed structure. The group from Fukuoka was incredulous. "No Japanese company would ever sell its flagship like that," explained Shuji.

A weaving pickup truck cut in front of our limousine; its driver honked and gave our Japanese driver the finger. Then, out of nowhere, a kid in a black Firebird roared past, swerved, and nearly sideswiped us. Every overpass, it seemed, was streaked with graffiti. If the Japanese guests were shocked by any of this, it didn't show. They giggled like schoolchildren and reached for the jar of hard candies on the bar. They were eager, they said, to see Trump Tower.

Having had six minutes to check into their rooms at the Plaza, the Fukuoka Endurance Players were back on the street. Shuji began the tour at Trump Tower; he would permit them about 10 minutes inside. Then five minutes in Tiffany's. Fifteen more in an apartment owned by a friend of Mitsui in Olympic Tower. Then swiftly by foot to Rockefeller Center, the AT&T Building, and finally, gloriously, to the Exxon Building—the flagship of Mitsui's overseas empire.

With Shuji in the lead, the group gathered momentum. At every corner, it seemed, he pointed up to some structure owned by the folks back home. The PaineWebber Building was owned by Nippon Life; the Tishman Building was owned by Sumitomo Real Estate; and the ITT Building by a maverick land assembler named Shuwa Corporation. And so on, until Shuji leaned over to me and said, "At the end of this tour, they will tell me how their necks hurt; they always say how their necks hurt from looking up." At one point I asked the bossy Fukuoka administrator what he thought of the tight tour schedule. "He said it doesn't matter the tightness of the schedule," said Shuji in translation, "just the fact that he has seen everything; he wants to go home and tell people he has seen all these things."

Truly, it is amazing the suffering these people are willing to endure for the sake of status. It was clear that the streets of New York caused the minds of our group members to fill with dread. No one wandered; no one strayed. As Shuji cut through the New York crowds, his right hand behind his back in the manner of the duke of Kent inspecting ball boys at Wimbledon, he sometimes lost the bossy administrator from Fukuoka. On these occasions the round man broke into a fast trot and once even ran through a red light. In four months in Tokyo, I had never seen a sober Japanese cross a street against the signal, although I'm told it has happened once or twice.

As the group zipped along, New Yorkers snickered at the funny little Japanese trying to snap pictures while on the run. Because Shuji had no interest in playing sheepdog to a group of intrepid wanderers, he used the Fukuokans' fear to keep them close. To discourage the portly administrator from lagging, he told the Fukuokans not to be bullied by the "wine-bottle gangs." The wine-bottle gangs are central to the Japanese mythology of New York. They supposedly bump into Japanese tourists, drop and break cheap bottles of wine, and scream for compensation. "They ask for their $50," said Shuji, "and the Japanese people give it to them!"

The victimization of Japanese by New Yorkers turned out to be one of Shuji's favorite subjects. The wine-bottle gangs seemed tame next to the taxi drivers who, if their meters read $37.50, made the gullible Japanese pay $375. And even the taxi divers were puffballs compared to the real estate tycoons. The way New York developers cheat Japanese investors is a recurring and engrossing subject among the Japanese. Around the end of 1987, when Japanese money began to flood New York, the developers discovered they could cut deals with these new investors that passed all of the financial risk and only part of the financial return to the Japanese. About this time, Mitsui first started looking at Manhattan properties. New York bankers and brokers began to appear with big brochures and promise Mitsui that, if it only handed its cash over to some developer, it would earn a minimum of 14 percent annual compounded return. The reality turned out to be not nearly so lucrative. "They lied to us," said Shuji, simply.

Then he pointed to a few of the bullets dodged by Mitsui— smaller disasters in and around Times Square: empty shells of buildings that started with Japanese money and ended in tears. Number One Broadway Place, on the corner of 44th and Broadway, had been erected for a fee by New York developer Eichner Property Management, using money from the Japanese construction company Hazama. It was in default. Another three had been built for a fee by Zeckendorf Properties, using money from C. Itoh and three Japanese real estate companies, Tobishima,

Kumagai-Gumi, and Kohnoiki Gumi. When Zeckendorf began to falter, Tobishima was forced to buy 50 percent of the company.

As we neared the Exxon Building, we stood not far from the site of the best-known tale of Japanese victimization in New York: 1133 Avenue of the Americas. Shuji didn't mention the gruesome particulars of the story; I learned of them from another source. The Japanese real estate and construction firm Kumagai-Gumi had formed a partnership with the New York developer called New York Land to erect an office building on the site. Kumagai-Gumi not only had agreed to put up all the money for construction, managed by New York Land, with no limit on changes, but also had guaranteed New York Land an enormous fee should the project be aborted for any reason. The initial budget for the entire project was $190 million. The building was meant to be finished by the summer of 1990.

By July 1990 the building stood half-finished, with construction halted, and it had already cost $220 million. Because of an onerous legal agreement, Kumagai-Gumi could not extract itself without paying to New York Land an exit fee of another $220 million. As the source of this tale put it, "Kumagai-Gumi is now going to Bernstein [the owner of New York Land] and saying, 'How much do I f——ing owe you to *leave me alone!*'" In early October, Kumagai-Gumi announced its plans to sell $1.5 billion of its foreign landholdings. So much for the myth that nothing short of a death threat can persuade a Japanese to sell his property and that the corollary Japanese assault on our national heritage is relentless.

The point of these examples isn't that all New York real estate developers are sharks—though, as far as I know, that could be true. The point is that America presents its own unsystematic obstacles to the Japanese. They are designed to separate the rich new player, the Japanese, from his cash. And they do. Shuji can tell stories all day long about cost overruns on construction financed by Japanese money. "If we wanted," said Shuji, "we could look at New York business practices as a kind of trade barrier." Or as an American employee of Mitsui put it to me, "For the Japanese, this place is a den of f——ing rattlesnakes." According to Shuji, no Japanese investor has made money yet in the New York real estate business.

"You're looking at one of our biggest priorities."

Dean Martin
Ramp Agent, Newark

At Federal Express, we don't just deliver documents and small packages
throughout the world. We also deliver big packages, big crates, and big containers
throughout the world. In a big hurry.

CHAPTER 5

WHY DO THE JAPANESE WANT TO LEAP INTO OUR SNAKE PIT?

It is easy to forget how recent are the massive purchases of American real estate by Japanese companies. Until 1986 no Japanese real estate company owned a building that could be considered a flagship, which, as a rule of thumb, is a prestigious building of at least one million square feet. Sellers often didn't even bother to offer large pieces of real estate to Japanese investors. As one man who makes his living selling American real estate to Japanese put it to me, "Between 1984 and 1987, there were all these deals being done that the Japanese weren't seeing because no one thought they were for real."

Then, late in 1986, Mitsui Real Estate made its first big purchase east of the Rocky Mountains. It paid $610 million for the Exxon Building. Soon thereafter, Mitsui announced its intention to invest 25 percent of its assets in properties outside Japan. In 1950 Mitsui had a net asset value of just 500 million yen. By 1970 that number had grown to a still modest 18 billion yen. Now, according to one report, the net asset value of Mitsui Real Estate is 3.1 *trillion* yen, or about $25 billion. The value of its overseas holdings is only 300 billion yen, or about 10 percent of its portfolio. To reach its target of 25 percent, Mitsui would need to purchase $3 billion worth of foreign property. And if history can serve as a guide, much of this would be in Honolulu, Los Angeles, and New York City.

There are all sorts of reasons for Mitsui to stay home, ranging from wine-bottle gangs to carnivorous New York dealmakers to hostile American politicians. And even though it is the second-largest property company in the world (behind Mitsubishi), Mitsui, unlike Toyota or Sony or Toshiba, doesn't need to reach outside Japan in search of markets. It doesn't depend upon foreign consumers for its profits. It could focus entirely upon domestic development.

What's more, Mitsui's overseas operations have, like those of every other Japanese real estate company, run consistently at a loss. People normally seek to build on success rather than on failure; certainly no American company would tolerate an overseas operation that consistently lost money. Everyone seems to agree that the Japanese drive to accumulate American real estate has a mysterious, almost suicidal quality. When Donald Trump was asked by *Time* magazine the value of his trophies, he replied, "Who the f—— knows? I mean, really, who knows how much the Japs will pay for Manhattan property these days?"

The explanation most widely believed to explain the Japanese eagerness to invest in American real estate is the one least often voiced: that somewhere in Japan the Japanese have a sinister master plan to buy the world. On the day after a fire at Universal Studios, for example, the London *Times* reported that people in Hollywood were "pointing the finger at the Japanese, who are bitterly resented since Sony Corporation bought Columbia Pictures for $3.4 billion earlier this year. MCA/Universal is the subject of an $8 billion takeover bid by Matsushita, the Japanese electronics giant, and as news of the fire reached New York and the film studio's share price dropped, some insiders said that the company might be bought up in the biggest fire sale in history." (On November 27, 1990, Matsushita bought MCA/Universal for more than $6 billion.)

This sort of anti-Japanese sentiment has been around since Japanese were first permitted to leave Japan in 1853, and is distilled in the poem that heads the previous chapter. The most commonly voiced view about Japanese investment, on the other hand, is that the Japanese are simply exploiting a strong yen. The strength of the yen may explain the start of the investment boom. It is true that Japanese purchases of foreign real estate soared with the yen after the Plaza Accord of 1985, in which finance ministers of the five leading industrialized nations agreed to weaken the U.S. dollar. But it doesn't explain the Japanese tendency to overpay, then hang around to absorb enormous losses.

There is no end to the hypotheses. Many people are willing to believe that the Japanese get taken for a ride simply because they are foolish. Others say that Japanese, unlike Americans, are long-term investors willing to lose in the short run because they expect their investments to pay off in the centuries ahead. This may be so, but there are better ways to make money in the long run than by overpaying in the short run. Still another explanation is that the Japanese expand their holdings regardless of price simply because they are able to: the money means nothing to them. Since shareholders in Japanese companies enjoy no rights, Japanese managers feel no pressure to make money or act wisely. The share price of Mitsubishi, for example, has fallen about 60 percent since its disastrous purchase of Rockefeller Center, and the only sound heard in Japan is not criticism from its shareholders (of whom, sadly, I am one) but laughter from its rivals.

I saw little to justify *any* of the answers commonly given to the question of why the Japanese are overrunning the New York property market. What logic I was able to discern in the Japanese Offense, at least in New York real estate acquisition, turned out to be far stranger and far less formidable. It had to do with status back in Japan.

When I asked Shuji why Mitsui bothered to expand, he said that to compete successfully in Japan, it needed to attract graduates from Japan's leading universities. "You cannot ask people who wear blue jeans and listen to Madonna to work for you," he said, "if you do not have an international business." There is more to this argument than meets the American eye. Japanese real estate firms find themselves precariously situated in the all-important quest for corporate prestige. As land prices in Japan have risen, the Japanese real estate trade has become uncomfortably linked to organized crime. Japanese law and custom favor tenants over landlords. Real estate firms have so often had to hire gangsters to pressure tenants to leave their homes and make way for development that a new line of criminals—called *jiageya*, or "land sharks"—has sprung up in Japan.

The association has ruined the reputation of real estate developers. As a surprisingly frank report from a French brokerage house put it: "A career in Japanese property is even less reputable than joining a stockbroker." As a result, nice young men from Japan's leading universities are less and less inclined to work in real estate. This causes a problem for Mitsui because the continual flow of squeaky-clean graduates from topflight schools is crucial to its all-important domestic business; only squeaky-clean graduates from the best schools can deal with Japanese government officials as equals and coax planning permission from them.

And Mitsui is particularly vulnerable to a dip in prestige. "It is the secret of Mitsui's postwar growth," continues the same brokerage report, "that it has more effectively than any other company taken advantage of this system [forcing reluctant tenants out of homes and shops to make way for development] while remaining distinct from it, at least on the surface. . . . If money is made by assembling plots large enough to warrant a change in planning permission . . . it matters enormously whether the company's negotiators went to the same university as the administrators. In Mitsui's case, they did; in other cases, they did not. No company has a record of favorable planning applications like Mitsui's."

So a Japanese real estate business needs educated elites for its domestic development, but the educated elites won't have anything to do with the sordid domestic real estate business—unless, of course, there is a prestigious foreign posting on the horizon. If that sounds farfetched, consider that Shuji himself—who was a star in Mitsui's domestic operation—probably would not have joined Mitsui had they not offered him the chance to work overseas.

The profit motive, says Shuji, is of secondary importance. Standing at a window in the Mitsui offices, he said, "To understand what's happened in Manhattan, you have to understand the mentality of the salaryman. You are young—30 years old. You work for Mitsui. You've got to do something before the Sumitomo guy does something. If it appears in the *Nikkei* [Japan's leading financial daily] that Sumitomo did their big deal, your company president will look at newspaper and say, 'What's Shuji Tomikawa doing there?'" To the salaryman, he explains, what is important is not money or profits but the avoidance of conspicuous failure. "Dai-Ichi suffers, Mitsubishi suffers, Mitsui suffers," says Shuji. "We all suffer together. That makes Japanese salarymen feel better . . . as long as no one firm is extremely profitable."

Of course, the fear of falling behind exists everywhere, but nowhere does it drive behavior as in Japan. (Lord knows how they handle puberty.) When Mitsui bought the Exxon Building, its chief *zaibatsu* rivals, Sumitomo and Mitsubishi, found themselves embarrassingly short of prestige. "Sumitomo had two guys who had been there six or seven years without buying anything," an investment banker central to the deal told me.

"They called and said, 'Look, we need something. And we need something *slightly* above Mitsui.'" Not long afterward, Sumitomo bought 666 Fifth Avenue (the building on the corner of 54th with the Barnes & Noble bookshop on the ground floor). It stood a block away from the Mitsui offices, like one of those tall, thin towers in San Gimignano from which medieval Italians poured excrement and boiling oil onto their rivals.

This left Mitsubishi staring up in envy. "Mitsubishi saw Mitsui and Sumitomo making statements," says an investment banker who often deals with Mitsubishi, "and they didn't have a statement." Which is to say that top executives of Mitsubishi in Japan had nothing to say for themselves.

Enter Rockefeller Center. On September 1, 1989, it was announced that all bids on the property must be submitted to Shearson Lehman, investment bankers to the Rockefeller Corporation, by November 15. We now know that representatives of the Rockefeller family discreetly approached Mitsubishi as much as 10 months earlier. But it wasn't until Mitsui declared its intention to bid on the property that Mitsubishi truly came to life. Not long after September 1, Mitsui Real Estate received a pair of visitors from Mitsubishi Bank. "They were so obviously spies for real estate," says one Mitsui employee. "They were trying to find out what we were going to do. So I told them we were going to start buying office space in Detroit."

The ensuing battle has gone largely unreported. Mitsubishi, which had no experience in New York property acquisitions, was at a disadvantage. Walk into the New York offices of Mitsui, and you see rows of computers used for valuation; Mitsubishi had none of these. Looking over their shoulders at archrival Mitsui, the managers of Mitsubishi hired a Texas company to evaluate Rockefeller Center on its behalf. Mitsui hired Goldman, Sachs in early October as a financial adviser; two days later Mitsubishi hired First Boston. Mitsui hired White & Case as a legal adviser; a few days later Mitsubishi hired Dewey Ballantine. Mitsui hired Arthur Young to be their accountants; a few days later Mitsubishi hired Ernst & Whinney, which had just merged with Arthur Young. Ernst & Whinney and Arthur Young claimed they had a Chinese wall between them so that they could serve two Japanese masters simultaneously.

In mid–October several days were set aside by Millbank Tweed, the attorneys of the Rockefeller family, during which bidders were allowed to photocopy thousands of important documents. A team from Mitsui showed up at the law firm's offices with five photocopiers; the team from Mitsubishi took 10. In New York on October 26 there was the semiannual convention of the Urban Land Institute, an association of real estate professionals. Mitsui, as always, sent its New York professionals. Mitsubishi, for the first time ever, did not. "They were trying to demonstrate how hard they were working on the Rockefeller Center project," said one source close to the rivalry. This was silly, since everyone at Mitsui knew that a team in Texas was doing all the work. "This wasn't a normal American-style corporate rivalry," said another real estate specialist who watched the process. "It had nothing to do with who made the most money. It had to do with the prestige of the company, with being the biggest. They were taking their backyard battle into the global market." The most publicized victory for the Japanese Offense—acquisition of Rockefeller Center—was actually a turf war.

The time to bid arrived early because a team from Mitsubishi preempted Mitsui and on October 29 offered $846 million for 51 percent of the Rockefeller shares; Mitsui, believing itself to be valuing the property generously, would have come in a distant second had it bid. Its offer would have been around $400 million. In the whole history of auctions, there would never have been such a dramatic difference between the first and second bids. Several people involved suggested that Mitsubishi put nearly half a billion dollars on the table simply because it feared losing the property to Mitsui. One Mitsui employee told me he felt Mitsui had been invited to bid merely to goad Mitsubishi. "It was a *wonderful* approach. We were a stalking horse," he said. "Mitsubishi's decision," one man involved with the sale told me, "was emotional rather than rational." Proving that Mitsubishi Estates overpaid for Rockefeller Center to avoid humiliation at the hands of its rivals is difficult. On the other hand, would anyone care to argue the opposing case?

One of the most bizarre consequences of the Rockefeller Center deal was that the flagship of Mitsui's overseas empire, the Exxon Building, is now managed by Mitsubishi even though it was not included in the purchase. Several employees of Mitsui complained to me that the trash had been piling up outside their building. The ground-floor staff, now effectively employed by

"あなたの街をとても良く知っている
フェデラル・エクスプレスです。"

Jun Funabashi
Courier, Tokyo

"When it comes to the international shipping business,
we know our way around like the natives. Because we *are* the natives."

Shuji and Yuki Tomikawa: a typical Japanese couple out shopping for skyscrapers in Manhattan.

Mitsubishi, had grown sluggish. And so on. I didn't actually see the evidence, but I'm not sure it matters. Suspicion without evidence is one of the recurring themes of the *zaibatsu* turf war.

The point of all this is simply that the logic of the Japanese Offense isn't exactly what you'd expect. Japanese companies, it seems, can be as perverse as the Fukuoka Endurance Players, chasing targets and goals without ever asking why and allowing business to become an elaborate status game. If there were a conspiracy afoot, then the issue of Japanese swarm tactics might be more easily addressed. But if America is being victimized by some coordinated Japanese assault, then it is a particularly badly coordinated assault—one far more damaging to Japan than to America. The aggressors spend all their time fighting each other. Mitsui builds one golf course for business and Mitsubishi another. Sony buys Columbia, and rival Matsushita pays top dollar for MCA. On and on it goes, benefiting those Americans who, starving for capital, want to sell assets. Just ask Donald Trump.

THE OTHER CAPITALISM

One of Shuji's favorite subjects is America. As a former chairman of the Japan-America student council, the creator of an annual trip of 100 Harvard Business School students to Japan, and a milker of cows in upstate New York, he has earned the right to criticize. He came to one of our meetings in a Japanese restaurant in Manhattan with an article from the British weekly *The Economist*. He said that the piece, called "America's Decadent Puritans," had touched a nerve in New York's Japanese community. The passage that he cited read as follows:

"The worry is about what might be called a 'decadent puritanism' within America: an odd combination of ducking responsibility and telling everyone else what to do. The decadence lies in too readily blaming others for problems, rather than accepting responsibility oneself."

I egged him on because it is rare that a Japanese businessman in America airs his views about America. On one occasion he grew so animated that his wife, Yuki, began to worry that I might be offended. Later she and I were standing outside their apartment behind the American Museum of Natural History, and Shuji, having just made some cogent remark about quality control in American manufacturing, had disappeared to retrieve his car. As we lingered on the subject of what's wrong with America, I pointed sheepishly to the vagrants on the museum benches. Yuki was wishing to change the subject. "Oh no," she said, "I think your homeless people are cleaner than ours."

The gist of Shuji's criticism was that America had once been a great place but threw it away with the liberalism of the '60s. "It was great for the individual," he said, "but at the same time it was a disaster." This view is quietly expressed all over Japan. I can't count the number of times some wizened Japanese industrialist said wistfully of the postwar period, "Ah, America was a great place *then*." Characteristically, Shuji put the case more strongly. "Sixties parents," he said, "will regret their entire lives when they die." There was in America, he said, too much freedom. Like a lot of Japanese, he thought Americans should rewind their body clocks to 1950. The implication was that if we did we could compete with Japan. In other words, there was nothing special about Japan that made it invincible. Japanese capitalism was simply capitalism as it was once practiced in America.

The Japanese cherish the 1950s brand of American capitalism epitomized by quality-control expert W. Edwards Deming.

This is one of the great themes emerging in Japanese-American relations: that America all of a sudden has something to learn from the Japanese—something we once knew but have forgotten; that Japan is now the normal capitalist country and America the deviant. Japanese executives never weary of telling you that their most cherished ideas about quality control came from an American expert named W. Edwards Deming, who went to Japan in 1950 with a faith in statistical concepts and an admiration of the Japanese. ("I was the only man in Japan in 1950," he later told an interviewer, "to believe my prediction that within five years manufacturers around the world would be screaming for protection; it took four.")

In many ways Japan does vaguely resemble 1950s America: the emphasis on *how* money is made rather than *how much* is made, the servile devotion of employees to their corporations, the emphasis on production rather than consumption, the mere fact of trade and capital surpluses. Most Japanese businessmen could be slipped unnoticed into the pages of one of those classic '50s books about conformism, such as *The Organization Man*. Similarly, much of the criticism of the American corporate mentality in the 1950s could just as easily be describing Japan today: "We have become less individualistic and less wrapped up in personal display," sociologist David Reisman wrote in 1953, "and we 'socialize' our abundant wealth by corporate display. Corporations vie with each other to have modern factories equipped with all manner of personal services, from masseurs to music by Muzak, and their advertisements increasingly sell not the product but the company's up-to-dateness in the arts of conspicuous production."

The analogy between America in the 1950s and Japan today

also suggests that Japan is simply a few years behind America on the evolutionary curve of capitalism, and that it, too, will become a decadent nation of sybarites. In Japan, this is the respectable view voiced by workaholics across the land. When I was in Osaka I heard a Japanese anthropologist explain that Japan had entered the fourth stage of capitalism (whatever that may be), with grave consequences for its social structure. He said the household unit (meaning both the corporation and the family) had given way to the individual as the basic building block of Japanese society. Fathers had lost control of their sons. With what the professor called the New Individualism would come a greater willingness to quit jobs, a new boom in consumption, and a dramatic decline in economic productivity.

If this is happening, there is precious little evidence. When pressed, the professor cited only the purchase of status goods such as Louis Vuitton luggage by Japanese women and the tendency of the younger generation in Japan to trade in the Shinto gods of their households for Shinto gods of their own. (It is customary for a Japanese family to worship household gods.) And if his case for the breakdown of the family was weak, the one for the breakdown of the principal Japanese household, the corporation, was ludicrous. The professor happily acknowledged that wages were rising at a much slower rate than corporate profits, that there was nothing like a free market in labor (many large Japanese companies have *never* had an employee leave to join a competitor), and that the Japanese consumer suffered to feed the Japanese producer.

Granted, it is perhaps a bit too easy for an American in Japan to spot the suppression of individual preferences: loudspeakers in the middle of nowhere blare shrill recordings of orders to do this and not to do that; lines of schoolchildren obey their teachers; pedestrians obey traffic signals even when there is no traffic. It requires all of one's self-control not to grab an obedient Japanese boy by the front of his black Prussian school jacket and shout instructions at him about spitballs, pigtails, and inkwells. And if one is in an especially Orwellian mood, the sight of Japanese businessmen falling asleep at every chance—on trains, in meetings, at baseball games, in the middle of conversations—might lead one to conclude that the citizenry is intentionally deprived of sleep so as to be rendered passive. So rather than posit some sinister controlling force, let us merely assume that Japanese are naturally exhausted and obedient. It's nicer that way. Still, the evidence is stacked overwhelmingly against the view that the Japanese are learning to assert themselves.

The *zaibatsu* are perhaps the most dramatic illustrations of the fact because they are premised on everyone's staying put in his place. Outside of standing armies, there is nothing anywhere in the industrial world to compare with these feudal empires. And because they are merely the institutional expression of the uniquely Japanese willingness to conform, it is no accident that these giant clusters of unrelated businesses have grown and grown, even as every other industrialized country has watched its conglomerates split into pieces and get sold. Last year, for the first time, the annual revenues of the collected companies in the Mitsubishi group surpassed $175 *billion* (compared with $127 billion grossed by General Motors). "What we are seeing," one student of the *zaibatsu* told *Business Week*, "is the Mitsubishification of the world." Whether or not this is true, no one in Japan is complaining as Mitsubishi comes to resemble more and more its prewar self, filled with Organization Men. Which is to say that the idea that the current Japanese economy is simply an earlier stage of capitalism than our own is misleading.

I simplify a bit. The company for which Shuji works is in some ways different from the prewar *zaibatsu*—but not in ways that encourage the independence of its employees. As Shuji points out, Japanese company executives before the war were able to become rich, whereas "Japanese company executives today can't get rich unless they take bribes." What's more, most of the *zaibatsu* family members were purged during the American Occupation. So an employee's loyalty lies no longer with the Mitsui family but with the Mitsui idea. These changes do nothing to loosen the corporation's grip on its employees. On the contrary, the worse the pay, the harder it is to become financially independent.

Some say the system will fail to accommodate the new generation of wealthy Japanese. Shuji, however, who comes from a wealthy family, is precisely the sort of person the professor of anthropology had in mind when he spoke of the New Individualism. He has all options before him. He thinks for himself. There is nothing inscrutable or sinister or submissive about him. Yet he has chosen to work for the most hierarchical and distinctively Japanese of institutions. His life is circumscribed by his company in a way that would have been surprising even for an Organization Man. He graduated from Keio University, which has fed Mitsui since the turn of the century. He met his wife, a former Mitsui office lady, at work. The videotape of their wedding reception at the Mitsui Club in Tokyo shows a succession of Mitsui executives standing and praising Shuji and Yuki for their contribution to Mitsui. After business school he declined the six-figure salaries offered by Wall Street firms and instead went to work for Mitsui for an amount well below six figures.

Shuji genuinely believes in the idea of a collective work effort. "You can call us a monolithic society," he says, "but isn't that homogeneity of brain necessary for an industrial society?" He grows emotional when he describes how the father of a Mitsui executive dies and 200 Mitsui executives travel 200 miles from Tokyo for the funeral. The need for the esteem of others, which in an American somehow finds its way into flashy cars and summer homes in Aspen, in Shuji is channeled into the improvement of Mitsui Real Estate. His greatest fear is being sent by Mitsui back to his old Tokyo neighborhood—which Mitsui now owns—to evict his boyhood friends from their homes; but he doesn't doubt that he'd do it.

I notice that I've gone on a bit about the system. Sorry. Somewhere along the way it became my personal obsession. Shuji found my rantings on the subject mildly insulting: "What! You think I didn't have complete control of my destiny?" Perhaps I'm wrong and Shuji is right and Japanese capitalism, despite all evidence to the contrary, has undergone profound change. There's no doubting that the current speculative boom has created for the first time a whole new class of people who don't associate wealth with industry and who can fly to America first class on their own rather than business class with Mitsui. There's also little doubt that they'd still rather work for Mitsui.

CONCLUSION

I t isn't surprising that in trying to identify patterns in the fabric of Japanese commerce I keep thinking about the structure of the economy, and especially the *zaibatsu*. After all, for the last two years American trade negotiators have called their discussions of Japanese trade barriers the Structural Impediments Initiative and have asked time and again for tougher enforcement of the antimonopoly laws. But the more I see of the Japanese system, the less inclined I am to criticize it. I mean, if neither Bob Collins, who has to be subjected to it, nor Shuji Tomikawa, who lives within it, see any need for changing it, who am I to complain?

American attitudes are distorted by the faith that, deep down, the Japanese want a society, and therefore an economy, modeled after our own. This is a curious view, when every important American-style change in Japan has been made while staring into the barrel of a gun or under the threat of American trade sanctions. Take away the gun and the threats and Japan reverts to its former self. As John Roberts, author of *Mitsui*, has written, "The effort of the Occupation to introduce free competition into Japan was one of the most quixotic episodes in economic history." The Japanese are not like us, and their economic system reflects the cultural differences.

The Japanese way of doing business isn't as intentionally threatening as the newspapers sometimes suggest. In some ways it would be better if there *were* a conspiracy in Japan to run enormous trade surpluses and buy the world. Addressing a xenophobic and irrational desire to exclude foreigners from the Japanese insurance markets, for example, would be easier than penetrating the tight web of interests that all too rationally preserves the status quo. For some quirks of the Japanese system we should be deeply grateful. Who knows how cheaply Rockefeller Center could have been bought had there not been a rivalry among the *zaibatsu* interests? (The same spirit of rivalry, by the way, could be seen when Matsushita announced its desire to purchase the media company MCA. The newspapers were filled with tortured explanations for why Matsushita would pay so much for the company. Another—or perhaps an additional—

explanation is that Sony had recently bought Columbia, and the rivalry between Matsushita and Sony is similar to that between Mitsui and Mitsubishi.) The system of government administration faced by Bob Collins—the divvying up of market share and maintaining the status quo—checks aggression in Japan. It doesn't operate quite as effectively overseas, where the rules haven't been established.

The misunderstanding between Japan and America cuts both ways. On my most recent trip to Tokyo, I was interviewed by the editor of the Japanese *Playboy* magazine. He wanted to speak with me to verify his suspicions about my former employer, Salomon Brothers. The Japanese stock market had fallen almost by half between the time I met Bob Collins and the time I met with the *Playboy* editor, and many Japanese were looking for someone to blame. The editor said that his "Deep Throat in the Ministry of Finance" had informed him that Salomon Brothers was responsible for the crash. Salomon Brothers, he said, was acting as an agent of the United States government to bring about the financial ruin of Japan. Anyone could see that. Salomon and the U.S. Treasury were in league, he said. Salomon was the largest distributor of U.S. Treasury bonds. And hadn't they hired David Stockman?

It is wrong to generalize too much from the experiences of two businessmen. But it is tempting, since each in his own way is a kind of paradigm. Bob Collins worked for one of the few American companies to succeed in Japan, yet even the senior executives of that enterprise admit that the success couldn't be repeated today. Shuji Tomikawa represents the new breed of wealthy, fun-loving Japanese, yet he still fits neatly into the Japanese economic machine. If anything, they incline one to worry about the future of relations between Japan and America. I could easily be wrong, but I'll bet the question in America will no longer be "How do we open Japan?" Instead it will become "How can *our* capitalism beat *their* capitalism?"

"We didn't just start an air express service. We started a revolution."

At Federal Express, we do a lot more than deliver packages and freight swiftly and dependably to more than 120 countries worldwide. We work in partnership with companies to design and operate the most sophisticated business logistics systems in the world. This allows companies to expand their markets, improve productivity, and compete more efficiently in a rapidly-changing global economy. You could call it revolutionary.

Additional Copies

To order additional copies of *Pacific Rift* for friends or colleagues, please write to The Larger Agenda Series, Whittle Direct Books, 505 Market St., Knoxville, Tenn. 37902. Please include the recipient's name, mailing address, and, where applicable, title, company name, and type of business.

For a single copy, please enclose a check for $11.95 payable to The Larger Agenda Series. When ordering 10 or more books, enclose $9.95 for each; for orders of 50 or more books, enclose $7.95 for each. If you wish to place an order by phone, call 800-284-1956.

Also available, at the same prices, are copies of the previous books in The Larger Agenda Series: *The Trouble With Money* by William Greider, *Adhocracy: The Power to Change* by Robert H. Waterman Jr., *Life After Television* by George Gilder, *The Book Wars* by James Atlas, *The X Factor* by George Plimpton, and *A Short History of Financial Euphoria* by John Kenneth Galbraith.

Please allow two weeks for delivery.
Tennessee residents must add 7¾ percent sales tax.